Speaking
in
Tongues

Speaking in Tongues

Larry Christenson

BETHANY HOUSE PUBLISHERS
MINNEAPOLIS, MINNESOTA 55438
A Division of Bethany Fellowship, Inc.

20th printing, 1987

Published by Bethany House Publishers
A Division of Bethany Fellowship, Inc.
6820 Auto Club Road, Minneapolis, Minnesota 55438

Printed in the United States of America

ISBN 0-87123-996-5

foreword

I praise the Lord for this book by the Rev. L. Christenson. I know that God will use it to open the eyes of many of His children to the privilege of living in a time when God is pouring out His blessings of the gifts and fruit of the Spirit on different churches, many which hitherto have been closed to these blessings.

The Lord did not in any way give His gifts as a means to quarrel about, but He gave His gifts that we should enjoy them.

As the Rev. Christenson said in his book:

"The gift of speaking in tongues and the other gifts of the Spirit are the means which He has given to express Christ's love in an effective and concrete way."

God bless this book.

Corrie ten Boom

preface
to the
20th anniversary edition

In 1961, as a newly ordained pastor, I stumbled upon the phenomenon of speaking in tongues. At first it did not particularly interest me. Several months later, however, I experienced the gift myself.

Inquiries—and controversy—were not far behind. The term "charismatic" had not been coined yet. The experience of speaking in tongues was generally unknown in mainline denominations. Pastors in neighboring communities and members of my own congregation began to ask questions. Nothing in my own religious tradition had prepared me for this.

Fortunately, nothing had prejudiced me against it either.

As I began to think through the experience, one Bible verse spoke to me with singular clarity:

> GOD HAS APPOINTED in the church, first apostles, second prophets, third teachers, then workers of miracles, then healers, helpers, administrators, SPEAKERS IN VARIOUS KINDS OF TONGUES" (1 Cor. 12:28).

God does all things well. He does not appoint foolish or unnecessary things, certainly not dangerous things, for His Church. What God has established does not need to be defended, nor can it be downgraded. Our task is rather to discover the purpose and meaning that God had in mind when He appointed this gift for His Church.

A seminary classmate heard about my experience and wrote me a letter. My answer to that letter became the beginning of this book. The letter grew into an article which was later published in booklet form and widely distributed in a variety of editions, including more than a dozen foreign language editions. Subsequently, Wartburg Seminary in Dubuque, Iowa, requested a series of lectures at its annual "Luther Academy." These lectures, together with the original article, provided the groundwork for this book.

Today, speaking in tongues is not the sheer novelty that it was twenty-five years ago. The charismatic renewal has become a worldwide, churchwide phenomenon. Not since the days of the Early Church has the gift of tongues become so widespread. Yet people are still asking many of the same questions that were first posed to me by that seminary classmate.

It is gratifying to know that *Speaking in Tongues*, approaching its third decade of publication, continues to be a help and encouragement to people. My prayer remains the same: that these chapters will help Christian people to come into both an understanding and a personal experience of a beautiful gift of the Holy Spirit.

Larry Christenson
Pentecost, 1987

acknowledgments

Acknowledgment is gratefully made to the many individuals who have corresponded and spoken with the writer over the past years in regard to the subject of this book, sharing their insights and personal testimonies, some of which are shared in the following pages. These have been of great personal help to the writer in preparing the chapters of this book.

We also gratefully acknowledge the permission of the following publishers and/or writers for permission to make brief quotations from their works:

From *Weymouth's New Testament in Modern Speech* by Richard Francis Weymouth, special arrangement with James Clarke & Company, Ltd. Reprinted with the permission of Harper & Row, Publishers, Inc., New York.

From *The Meaning of Persons* by Paul Tournier, copyright 1957 by Paul Tournier, Harper & Brothers. Reprinted with the permission of Harper & Row, Publishers, Inc., New York.

From *Tongue Speaking* by Morton Kelsey, published by Doubleday, Inc., New York. Reprinted by permission of the author.

From *The Historic Church Newsletter*, Box 3743, Portland, Oregon 97208, the article entitled "Guidelines in the Present Movement" by Clarence Finsaas. Quoted by permission.

From *History of the Christian Church* by Philip Schaff, published by Wm. B. Eerdmans Publishing Company, Grand Rapids, Michigan. Used by permission.

From *Gnadengaben* by Arnold Bittlinger, published

by R. F. Edel Verlag, Madburg/Lahn, Germany. Quoted by permission of the author.

From *Christianity Today*, article by Philip Hughes. Quoted by permission.

From *Renewal Magazine*, article entitled "Pray, Don't Condemn!" Quoted by permission of the editor, Michael Harper.

From *The Normal Christian Church Life* by Watchman Nee, published by International Students, Inc., 2109 E. Street N.W., Washington, D.C. Quoted by permission.

From *The Biblical Expositor*, the article entitled "The Coming of Christian Power" by John H. Gestner, edited by Carl F. H. Henry, published by A. J. Holman Company. Quoted by permission.

From *The Healing Gifts of the Spirit* by Agnes Sanford. Quoted by permission of the author.

From *The New York Times*, article by McCandlish Phillips. Quoted by permission of the author.

From *The Young Church in Action* by J. B. Phillips, published by The Macmillan Company. Quoted by permission.

From the *Revised Standard Version* of the Bible, copyright 1946 and 1952 by the Division of Christian Education of the National Council of Churches. Quoted by permission.

contents

11

1

what does this mean?

*The Significance for the Church of the Current Wide-
spread Occurrence of SPEAKING IN TONGUES in
Historic Denominations*

A Typical Testimony

As a young teen-ager I accepted Christ's forgiveness, received salvation, and was baptized. This experience did not give me the ability to completely rely
on God. I sought security elsewhere, but there remained
an empty incompleteness, finally a despair. I turned
to God in helplessness. He met me by increasing my
faith and hope slowly.

I attended a prayer group obediently for a year
and a half, longing for a closer walk that would enable
me to experience the things which the Bible says a
Christian should experience. Again God answered my
prayers: through the testimonies of others and searching God's Word, His Spirit convicted me to humble
myself to ask for prayer to be baptized with His Spirit,
and take that step of faith necessary to receive Him. I
did, with the Lord's help, and He granted me a
tongue with which I could praise Him continually.

I have experienced a super abundance of joy and
peace and comfort that no one can take away from
me. . . . He also makes me painfully aware of 'myself'

that offends and hinders His growth in me. How
blessed to confess these things, be cleansed, and granted
more strength to stand. The enemy is more real, too,
but through God's Word, which has come alive, Christ
sets me free from Satan's power. . . .

He is my Comforter, as His language of prayer
and praise flow through my mind silently at any time,
anywhere, in any situation; or aloud, through my lips
and voice, when alone. . . . God speaks to me everywhere: in the liturgy, hymns, sermons, Scripture. His
Spirit witnesses to the truth I feel in my heart. I long
that all may share this blessed oneness in Christ Jesus
who sustains us in His power.

RETURN OF THE CHARISMATA*

The details will differ. One testifies to a new joy
in his Christian Faith; another witnesses to a deeper
and more constant awareness of the Spirit's indwelling
presence; some have found a new freedom to witness
to others of what Jesus means to them; another says
that he has a far keener sense of the Spirit's guidance
than he did before; many testify to an awakened interest, indeed a deep hunger, to study the Bible; a keener
awareness of one's own sins and shortcomings is frequently mentioned. The common denominator in all
of these testimonies seems to be this: The experience
of "speaking in tongues" has intensified the sense of
the presence of God; the Word of God has become
more contemporary, believable; Christ the Lord has
become more real—in a word, *faith has been strength-
ened.*

---

* The words **charismata** and **charismatic** are frequently heard in connection
with speaking in tongues. They come from the Greek word **charisma**, which
means 'gift' or 'favor,' and is especially used in the New Testament to
denote a gift of the Holy Spirit (I Cor. 12:9ff.; Rom. 12:6ff.).

A teacher of a high school Bible class came into this experience, and several months later one of his students remarked, "He's *changed*: he believes it more now than he used to." This is not the kind of change one learns out of a book. It springs from deep personal experience. This teacher does not make any extravagant claims in regard to his own experience. "I realize," he says, "that many people have come into blessings similar to mine without speaking in tongues. But this is the way God chose to lead me into a deeper walk with Him, and I thank Him for it."

What is "speaking in tongues"? Why has it begun to appear in many historic Christian denominations? Why haven't we heard about it before? What kind of an experience is it? Is it something any Christian can experience? Should one seek after it? Is it some kind of gimmick, which could detour the Church from her main task of proclaiming the Gospel? What, exactly, is its value to the individual and to the Church?

These are thoughtful and earnest questions which people in many Christian congregations are asking. Until recent years the average church member has associated present-day speaking in tongues with the so-called Pentecostal groups, often dismissing it as a purely emotional phenomenon. But in recent years an increasing number of people in historic Christian denominations—clergy and laity alike—have come into this New Testament experience.

However we may analyze or explain it, we cannot escape the fact that traditional church people now numbering in thousands and perhaps millions—Episcopalians, Presbyterians, Roman Catholics, Lutherans, Baptists, Methodists, to name a few—witness to having experienced this New Testament phenomenon. National magazines, both secular and religious, have carried articles on it.

McCandlish Phillips, in a feature article for *The New York Times*, wrote, "A movement emphasizing a restoration of 'charismatic' or spiritual gifts to the Christian ministry has lately been spreading through the nation's Protestant denominations. It is marked, among other things, by glossolalia or praying in unknown tongues.

"Glossolalia is the practice of praying, singing or speaking in fluent accents whose meaning is not known to the speaker.

"Across the United States, hundreds of ministers and thousands of laymen in about 40 denominations have adopted this strange prayer form. Most of them have also begun to practice a variety of other spiritual 'gifts,' especially healing by prayer with the laying on of hands.

"These and other phenomena are part of a random but pervasive movement called The Charismatic Renewal. . . . Its recent appearances in such august settings as the Protestant Episcopal Church and Yale University have caused Protestants to take a rather startled new look at the phenomenon.

"The movement had already gained a foothold in a score of seminaries and colleges when word was published last year that 19 Yale students, including graduate students with Phi Beta Kappa keys, were praying in tongues and finding it meaningful.

"At Princeton Theological Seminary, 20 students claim to have had direct experiences with the charismata and another 35 attend student meetings at which they are exercised."

Rev. Arnold Bittlinger, Director of Evangelism and Stewardship for the Lutheran Church of the Pfalz, Germany, encountered the phenomenon during a study-tour of American churches, under the auspices of the

Lutheran World Federation. His official report carried the following comments:

"During my stay in America, in different Lutheran churches I came across a new kind of Spiritual Awakening, in which the New Testament charismatic signs have come into evidence, and are practiced with great discipline and order. I had opportunities to take part in different worship services in which these gifts of the Spirit were in evidence. I was impressed with the solemn, liturgical beauty of these services. Everywhere they hold themselves strictly to the instructions of the Apostle Paul in I Corinthians 14:26ff.

"The life of the congregation is made fruitful in unexpected ways. That which otherwise functions through excellent organization, occurs among those involved in the Awakening very spontaneously and independently. The members of the congregation visit one another, they manifest a personal concern for those outside the Church, they pray for the sick, and they contribute their money and their time to the ministry of the Church. A pastor pointed out to me that one of these congregations which has experienced the Awakening had shown a new recognition of social problems, and set about solving them.

"One of the chief impressions is the ecumenical disposition of the Movement. For instance, one Lutheran congregation had refused to join the newly formed American Lutheran Church. They were determined to remain as an independent congregation. After this congregation had experienced some of the effect of the Awakening, the same members of the congregation who had been most strongly opposed to joining the ALC, voted to join it. The congregation today belongs to the ALC. It was also gratifying that I nowhere found evidence of legalism or undisciplined enthusiasm (*Schwaermerei*); on the contrary, the teaching of the

Confessions, especially the doctrine of 'grace alone,' infant baptism, and the Lord's Supper have found among these 'awakened Lutherans' a new and deeper meaning."

In a day when serious historians are beginning to characterize our times as the "post-Christian era," we see this strange counter-phenomenon: the return of the *charismata*. People in significant numbers are turning to the Bible and personally experiencing some of the phenomena which marked the origins of Christianity.

We would serve the Church ill to whisk these manifestations aside without a hearing, slapping on it the label of 'fad' or 'emotionalism.' And especially is this true here, for it does not involve merely a new church 'program,' 'approach,' or 'technique': *It involves a supernatural manifestation of the Holy Spirit which is clearly spoken of in the Bible.* This is holy ground, where a snap judgment or an ill-informed opinion could truly grieve the Spirit. One even writes about it with some qualms. But where silence runs the danger of conceding the day to fear and uniformed prejudice, one should speak. So, in the spirit of a Christian brother, and a fellow searcher of God's Word, I would share with you my understanding of speaking in tongues— *and its significance for the Church*—as it has come to me in prayer, study of the Bible, and experience over the past years.

What Is 'Speaking in Tongues'?

The Bible tells us that speaking in tongues is a manifestation of the Holy Spirit (Acts 2:4, 10:46, 19:6; I Cor. 12:10). St. Paul warns that the tongue can have a false note—like a noisy gong or a clanging cymbal—if the speaker does not manifest the gift *in love* (I Cor. 13:1); it may be used out of turn (I Cor.

14:27), or at the wrong time (I Cor. 14:28). But not even in Corinth, where tongues were greatly abused, does St. Paul suggest that it has degenerated into a purely human phenomenon, the product of excess emotionalism. His plea, rather, is that precisely because this *is* a manifestation of the Holy Spirit, it should be manifested "decently and in order" (I Cor. 14:40), for "God is not a God of confusion but of peace" (I Cor. 14:33). He does not tell them to *stop* manifesting this gift. On the contrary, he tells them to *continue manifesting the gift* (I Cor. 14:5a), but in a proper way (I Cor. 14:13, 28), and with a proper regard for the other manifestations of the Spirit as well (I Cor. 14:5b).

This must be the framework for any biblical discussion of speaking in tongues. We want to seek a clearer understanding and appreciation of the purpose the Spirit has in manifesting this gift in the Church. We dare never lose sight of the fact that speaking in tongues is a manifestation of the Holy Spirit. We miss St. Paul's point altogether if we begin to search out reasons why we should *not* speak in tongues, why we *don't* need this gift in the churches today, how much better we can do *without* it, and so on. It is well to be alert to the dangers of abuse which St. Paul points out, but we cannot depreciate the gift as such, for it is of the Holy Spirit. Scripture simply does not support an argument *against* speaking in tongues—only against its abuse. When once we grasp this basic truth, our whole discussion of tongues is cast in the positive framework which St. Paul himself reflects when he says, "I thank God that I speak in tongues more than you all" (I Cor. 14:18). The cure for abuse is not *dis*use, but *proper* use.

Now what, specifically, is the nature of this manifestation of the Spirit called "speaking in tongues"?

On the Day of Pentecost, the dwellers in Jerusalem

heard the Galilean believers speaking a variety of Mediterranean and Near Eastern dialects. They were amazed, just as you would be amazed if you were an American-born Jew who had returned to Israel and heard an uneducated Jew from Yemen begin to speak English with a Brooklyn accent!

Some commentators suggest that this was God's way of breaking the language barrier, so that the Gospel could be proclaimed to all nations. But this is unlikely, since there was no language barrier in Jerusalem on the Day of Pentecost. The men who heard the believers speaking in tongues had become permament residents* of Jerusalem, and were Jews besides, so they all had at least one language in common, and possibly two.

It would be a situation similar to a group of Norwegian immigrants living in South Dakota who suddenly hear some migrant field hands speaking the various dialects of Norway. There is no language barrier, since all could speak English (the Jews in Jerusalem could all speak Aramaic, and doubtless Greek as well), but the sight of migrant field hands speaking perfect Norwegian would certainly fill those immigrants with amazement!

The tongues were given not primarily as a means of communicating the Gospel, but as a *supernatural sign* that God was in the midst of these believers. This is doubly witnessed to in what follows: Peter immediately stands up and begins preaching to this same crowd (Acts 2:14ff.), and not in tongues, but obviously in a language which they all had in common.

In Corinth Paul says that those who spoke in

---

* The word in Greek is **katoikountes**, indicating Jews who had come to live in Jerusalem, though it is clear from the context that they were born elsewhere.

tongues were not understood (I Cor. 14:2). But the implication is not that they were speaking gibberish or ecstatic speech, but in languages not known to any of the fellow worshippers (I Cor. 14:10, 11).

Some commentaries have tried to establish an essential difference between the various occurrences of speaking in tongues in the New Testament, e.g., between the occurrence on the Day of Pentecost and the experience in the Corinthian Church. It would seem, however, that the manifestation of tongues in Acts and in Corinthians is essentially the same. In his *History of the Christian Church* (Vol. 1, pages 230–231), Philip Schaff says, "The glossolalia (speaking in tongues) on the Day of Pentecost was, as in all cases where it is mentioned, *an act of worship and adoration*, not an act of teaching and instruction, which followed afterwards in the sermon of Peter. The Pentecostal glossolalia was the *same* as that in the household of Cornelius in Caesarea after his conversion, which may be called a Gentile Pentecost, as that of the twelve disciples of John the Baptist at Ephesus, where it appears in connection with prophecy, and as that in the Christian congregation at Corinth."

The difference on the Day of Pentecost was not in the essential nature of the manifestation itself. It was rather that God, for a special purpose, on this occasion gave the believers languages which would be understood by the bystanders. In Christian congregations, such as the one at Corinth, God gave languages which were not generally understood.

This is borne out by present-day experience as well. A speaker in tongues is seldom understood. (In a group meeting his utterance will be 'interpreted,' but 'interpretation' is also a manifestation of the Spirit, and is not the same as translating a foreign language with the mind.) Occasionally people report an experi-

ence similar to that which occurred on the Day of
Pentecost: Someone speaks in tongues, and the utterance is understood by another as a known language—
though the speaker himself did not know the language
nor understand what he was saying.

Doesn't the speaker himself know what he is saying? No, to his own ear and understanding it is simply
a stream of sounds. St. Paul says specifically, "If I
pray in a tongue, my spirit prays *but my mind is
unfruitful*" (I Cor. 14:14). When you speak your
native tongue, or any language which you have consciously learned, your mind controls what is said. But
speaking in tongues is a speaking forth prompted not
by the mind, but by the Spirit. The speaker does not
'decide' what sound will come out next: He simply lifts
up his voice, and "the Spirit gives utterance" (Acts
2:4).

*Thus speaking in tongues is a supernatural mani-
festation of the Holy Spirit, whereby the believer speaks
forth in a language which he has never learned, and
which he does not understand.*

Is It Really a Language?

A woman in our congregation had never heard
anyone speak in tongues. When she went to a meeting
where someone spoke out in tongues, she leaned to
the person next to her and whispered, "That man is
drunk!"

This is a rather natural reaction. Not understanding
an utterance, one jumps to the conclusion that the
speaker is mumbling a drunken gibberish. That is exactly what happened on the Day of Pentecost.

John Gerstner, writing in *The Biblical Expositor*,
plausibly re-constructs the scene as follows: "As the
disciples waited in Jerusalem, according to the Lord's

command, they were baptized with the Holy Spirit (Acts 2:2, 3). A rushing wind was heard, tongues descended, and one rested on each of them and all began to speak. On the day of Pentecost, people from the entire Dispersion scattered all around the Mediterranean area were present. To these different language-speaking groups the Christians began to speak. In one such group, standing near Thomas perhaps, several different native dialects were spoken, none of which Thomas knew. But as he spoke, some of these people realized that he was speaking in their language even though he had never learned it. Those who understood Thomas were amazed to hear him speaking in their own languages; others in the group may have thought he was speaking some kind of gibberish. Meanwhile, Philip was speaking in another area, and the same thing was happening. Some understood him speaking in their own language; others thought he was mad or drunk (Acts 2:4–13)."

The point of this interpretation is that people jump rather too quickly to the conclusion that a person is speaking gibberish simply because they themselves do not understand it. This writer had the opportunity to visit with Professor Eugene Rapp, world-famous linguist at the University of Mainz, Germany. He speaks some 45 languages and is a specialist in West African dialects. He gave me a practical demonstration of coming into contact with a completely unfamiliar language. He read some lines out of one of his recent works: The Gospel of John in the language of a small West African tribe. To my unschooled ear it sounded like little more than a series of animal grunts. I have never heard any speaking in tongues which sounded so primitive. If I had heard sounds like that in a prayer meeting, I might have been tempted to dismiss it as gibberish. Yet this was a known language of earth.

The fact of the matter is, even a trained linguist cannot determine whether a brief utterance of unfamiliar sounds is in fact a language. Professor Rapp said: "I have once in my life heard someone speak in tongues. My impression was that it was no nonsense or gibberish. However, one cannot determine that from hearing just a few sentences. I would need at least sixteen pages of phonetically transcribed script to study and analyze before I could make a certain judgment." People who cavalierly dismiss speaking in tongues as "gibberish" speak out of ignorance. If a trained linguist cannot make that judgment, certainly a layman in the field could not.

Another common misconception is that speaking in tongues is a highly emotional or "ecstatic" utterance. The terms "ecstatic utterance" or "tongues of ecstasy" are *never* used in the Bible in reference to a speaker in tongues. Those who *hear* a speaker in tongues are sometimes described as "ecstatic" or "amazed" (*existanto*, Acts 2:7; *exestesan*, Acts 10:45), but the speaker himself is *never* described in this way. These misleading terms occur frequently in commentaries, and even turn up in translations of the Bible. The original text of the Bible gives no basis for such a translation. It seems to stem from an assumption on the part of the commentators and translators, who perhaps have not had the experience and therefore are at a disadvantage in describing its subjective aspects. There is nothing in the nature of speaking in tongues which is *per se* "ecstatic." It is, as the Bible so accurately puts it, simply a "speaking." It has the same emotional potential (and the same possibility of self-control!) as speech or prayer in one's native tongue. The terms "ecstatic utterance" and "tongues of ecstasy" are misleading and are not biblical.

Since speaking in tongues was a widely shared experience in the Early Church, no definition or explanation of the term was necessary. It was, as Bauer's Greek lexicon points out, a "technical term": The original readers of Mark, Acts, and First Corinthians would know at once what was meant, from their own experience.

Several variations of the term occur: *new* tongues (Mark 16:17), *other* tongues (Acts 2:4), *divers* tongues (I Cor. 12:10), *unknown* tongues (I Cor. 14:2). These variations seem to be more-or-less synonymous, expressing no essential difference in the phenomenon. The essence of the phenomenon is this: *The Holy Spirit gives the believer the power to speak a tongue or language which he has never before learned* (cf. Acts 2:5–8).

It is not enough, however, simply to refute the misconceptions that speaking in tongues is "gibberish" or "ecstatic utterance." The whole question of language should be looked at from another point of view.

Webster lists two basic meanings for the word "language":

1. The body of words and methods of combining words used and understood by a considerable community; a tongue.
2. Any means, vocal or other, of expressing or communicating feeling or thought.

The first definition clearly does not describe the phenomenon of speaking in tongues, in any practical sense. Even if we concede that a speaker in tongues is speaking an intelligible language, the fact of the matter is that it is understood neither by himself nor by those around him. In this 'community,' it does not serve as a means of communication. This is what St. Paul is getting at when he says, "There are doubtless many different languages in the world, and none is without meaning; but if I do not know the meaning of the language, I shall be a foreigner to the speaker and the speaker a foreigner to me" (I Cor. 14:10–11).

When we look at the second definition, however, we find a highly accurate definition of speaking in tongues. It defines language in terms of the speaker: *Language is an expression of meaning in terms of feeling or thought.* If speaking in tongues expresses the meaning of the speaker, then it is a language, according to this accepted definition.

A semanticist told a friend of mine, "No sound is without meaning." A sigh has meaning. A grunt has meaning. The la-la ditty which a child sings at play has meaning. A sudden ejaculation using a hitherto unknown word has meaning. The basic question we must ask is this: "Does speaking in tongues express meaning for the speaker?"

In *The Healing Gifts of the Spirit*, Agnes Sanford takes it a step further; she quotes a psychiatrist who said, "It can be a spiritual power entering into a person with such force that it reaches and touches something in the deep unconscious; whereupon the person speaks a language which the conscious mind does not know, but which this deep area of the unconscious does know."

Paul Tournier suggests much the same thing in his book, *The Meaning of Persons*: "Glossolalia, or speaking in tongues, which played such an important part then, and which is still found in some modern communities, appears to answer the need of the spirit to *express the inexpressible,* to carry the dialogue with God beyond the narrow limits of clearly intelligible language."

The Bible says that speaking in tongues is addressed to *God* (I Cor. 14:2). Therefore the question of whether *people* understand it is actually irrelevant. The question is: Does it express meaning for the speaker, and does God understand it?

Purely intellectual utterances are only one band of the spectrum of meaning, as we have suggested. It is altogether reasonable that something as deep and intimate as our relationship with God should find expression in supra-rational utterance—utterance which would express shades of feeling and thought beyond the capability of ordinary speech. Yet to God, who can discern our innermost thoughts, these utterances would be perfectly understandable.

It is in this sense that the Bible designates this phenomenon a *language* (the term *glossa* in Greek may be translated either "tongue" or "language," as also in English we speak of one's "mother tongue" when we mean language). Speaking in tongues is therefore speaking in a language—a language which expresses the deep feelings and thoughts of the speaker, a language which God hears and understands.

WHAT IS THE VALUE OF SPEAKING IN TONGUES?

Those who have experienced this manifestation of the Spirit find that it has great blessing and value. It is no 'frill' or 'extra' in their Christian life—something which they could now take or leave depending upon their mood. It has had a deep, often a transforming effect on their spiritual life. One man expressed it this way: "Speaking in tongues was a spiritual breakthrough for me." There is an awareness of having entered a vast new spiritual realm. And this leads to deeper study of the Scriptures, for one wants to know more about this realm which has suddenly taken on new reality. One suddenly finds himself able to understand the Bible far better. One young worker who received this experience said, "For years I have tried to force myself to read the Bible, but I never got anything out of it—I couldn't seem to understand it. Now I read the Bible every day, and I always get some new thought or insight."

One speaks in tongues, for the most part, in his private devotions. *This is by far its most important use and value.* It offers the believer a glorious new dimension in prayer. How often we come to the point where "we know not how to pray as we ought" (Rom. 8:26) ... where our mind can find no words to express the praise and love and adoration we feel toward God—

> *"What language shall I borrow*
> *To thank Thee, dearest Friend,*
> *For this Thy dying sorrow,*
> *Thy pity without end?"*

Often a burden of intercession simply overwhelms or baffles us. Then and there a person may pray in tongues, knowing that "the Spirit intercedes ... according to the will of God" (Rom. 8:27).

Although one does not know what he is saying as he speaks in tongues, he does have a clear sense that he is praying to God. The heightened awareness of God's presence is one of the greatest blessings one receives through this experience. A seventy-year-old pastor who came into this experience said, "Christ has never before been so real to me!"

While praying in tongues is itself a great joy and blessing to the believer, the more important blessings are those which *result* from praying in tongues. Paul sums it up by saying, "He who speaks in a tongue edifies himself" (I Cor. 14:4). While you are praying in tongues—or perhaps we should say, *through* your praying in tongues—the Spirit begins to work a great many changes in your life. You find yourself becoming far more aware of spiritual realities. Without a great deal of conscious effort, you find your thoughts becoming more and more filled with Jesus. You find a new ease and joy in witnessing.

WHY HAVEN'T WE HEARD ABOUT THIS BEFORE?

It's natural for us to wonder, "Why haven't we heard about this before, if it's such a blessing? Why is this suddenly happening now?" I imagine people raised the same kind of questions when Luther began to uncover truths of Scripture which had been long neglected. It is the kind of question to which we can give no final answer.

Perhaps we have simply neglected part of the biblical revelation, for speaking in tongues is clearly set forth in Scripture as a blessing and enduement from God. It was widely manifested in the Apostolic Church, and from time to time in Church History down to our own day.

But perhaps it goes deeper. Perhaps it is simply "God's time." In the unfolding plan of Redemption and Consummation, God's sovereign Spirit begins to move, calling into service a gift which He has allowed to slumber for a time. And we are not asked to apologize or atone for the past, but simply to respond to God's move in our own time.

In the following pages we want to consider two things:

1. The teaching of the Bible concerning the experience of speaking in tongues.
2. The practical application of this experience in the life of the individual and of the Church.

2

speaking in tongues
as 'sign'

The Significance of Speaking in Tongues As It Occurs in the Book of Acts, As an Aspect of the Baptism with the Holy Spirit

The first time that we encounter the phenomenon of speaking in tongues is in the Book of Acts, on the Day of Pentecost. The Holy Spirit had manifested himself in a variety of ways during Old Testament times and in the ministry of Jesus. In First Corinthians, Paul lists nine manifestations or *charismata* of the Holy Spirit. As we read through the list, we discover that all of these manifestations have precedence in the Old Testament or the Gospels—wisdom, knowledge, faith, healing, miracles, prophecy, discernment of spirits, even interpretation, when Daniel was able to interpret the handwriting on the wall—all except speaking in tongues.* Historically, speaking in tongues is uniquely related to the work of the Holy Spirit in and with the Christian Church. It is apparently a gift which He reserved for the Church.

---

* Arnold Bittlinger, in his book **Gnadengaben** (British edition published by Hodder and Stoughton, London, under Title "Gifts and Graces"), a commentary on I Corinthians 12–14, makes a case for the possibility that this gift is alluded to both in the Old Testament and in the Gospels. He concludes, however, "We cannot with certainty determine (whether people in the Old Testament, and Jesus, spoke in tongues)."

What was the Lord's intention in bestowing this gift upon His Church? The Book of Acts contains not a single theological statement or precept in reference to speaking in tongues. It simply records the *occurrence* of the phenomenon. But as we look into it, we discover that the occurrences are not random or arbitrary. They occur according to a definite pattern, and this pattern has significant implications for our understanding of speaking in tongues.

This is both a valid and helpful method of interpreting Scripture. The hermeneutical principle is well stated by Watchman Nee, in the Introduction to his book, *The Normal Christian Church Life*: "Christianity is built not only upon precepts but also upon examples. God has revealed His will not only by giving orders but by having certain things done in His Church, so that in the ages to come others might simply look at the pattern and know His will. God has directed His people not only by means of abstract principles and objective regulations but by concrete examples and subjective experience. God does use precepts to teach His people, but one of His chief methods of instruction is through history. God tells us how others knew and did His will, so that we, by looking at their lives, may not only know His will but see how to do it, too. He worked in their lives, producing in them what He himself desired, and He bids us look at them so that we may know what He is after."

What kinds of examples of speaking in tongues do we find in the Book of Acts? It is mentioned three times: Acts 2:4, on the Day of Pentecost; Acts 10:45, in the household of Cornelius, about 12 years after Pentecost; Acts 19:6, in Ephesus, about 24 years after Pentecost. The most striking similarity is that in each case the speaking in tongues is directly connected with an initial outpouring of the Holy Spirit upon a group of believers.

A variety of terms is used to describe the experience. It is referred to prophetically by John the Baptist and by Jesus as a *baptism* with the Holy Spirit; believers are described as being *filled* with the Spirit; Peter refers to it as the *gift* of the Holy Spirit; the Spirit is described as *falling* or *coming upon* the believers; believers are asked, "Did you *receive* the Holy Spirit when you believed?"

All of these expressions point to the same essential experience, which is the establishing of a new and dynamic relationship between the believer and the Holy Spirit. Within the framework of the Book of Acts, "Baptism with the Holy Spirit" is perhaps the most satisfactory term for this experience. All four Gospels record John the Baptist's prophetic use of this term; Jesus used it in anticipation of Pentecost; Peter applied the same term to the event in Cornelius' household twelve years later, indicating its general acceptance in the Apostolic Community. The baptism with the Holy Spirit was the fulfillment of "the promise of the Father" (Luke 24:49, Acts 1:4). God the Father made the promise in these terms to and through John the Baptist (John 1:33).

In the Book of Acts, it is the experience of the baptism with the Holy Spirit which provides the key to understanding the purpose and function of speaking in tongues, because all references to speaking in tongues occur in connection with it. In other words, it is as an aspect of this experience of the baptism with the Holy Spirit that speaking in tongues derives its significance in the Book of Acts. In order to understand speaking in tongues, we have to see exactly what Scripture outlines concerning the baptism with the Holy Spirit.

THE BAPTISM WITH THE HOLY SPIRIT

Before Jesus began His ministry, the Father sent a forerunner to announce His coming, and this was John the Baptist. He baptized people with water unto repentance. The Gospels record that he also baptized Jesus.

When we read about this, our processes of reason immediately go into action, and we ask ourselves, "Why did Jesus need to be baptized? Wasn't he born without sin, and didn't He live a sinless life? What need did He have to repent?"

As a matter of fact, this very idea is put into the mouth of Jesus himself in an apocryphal writing called "The Gospel to the Hebrews." In this book, the mother and brothers of Jesus urge Him to go with them to be baptized by John. But Jesus says to them, "Wherein have I sinned, that I should go to be baptized by him?"

Although this writing was never accepted into the canon of Scripture, we can nevertheless learn something from it. It shows us the natural workings of the human mind when it encounters divine truth. First of all, it tries to bring the divine truth within the scope of its own reason and understanding: "It's as simple as adding two and two. John's baptism is a baptism unto repentance. Jesus doesn't have any sin to repent of. Therefore Jesus doesn't need the baptism. What could be more reasonable?" The second step is to get God to go along with your own logical conclusions. So this writer of "The Gospel to the Hebrews," not having any authoritative Scripture to correct him, just makes up the words and puts them into Jesus' mouth. Completely logical. Completely reasonable. And completely false, because it just did not happen that way.

How it *did* happen is recorded in Matthew 3:11–17. "Then Jesus came from Galilee to the Jordan to

John, to be baptized by him. John would have prevented him, saying, 'I need to be baptized by you, and
do you come to me?' " John was a logical thinker, too.
His mind went through the same logical process: "I
baptize with water unto repentance. He has no sin.
Therefore I should not baptize Him. If anything, He
should baptize me!" Good reasoning. Completely logical, and with a touch of honest humility to boot. But
this very human reaction has one fatal flaw: It does
not conform to the Word and will of God.

Jesus, discerning what God's will is, says, "Let it
be so, now. —All of your thinking, John, is true
enough, but *nevertheless*, let it be so now." God's plan
and God's ways are bigger than human logic and
understanding. "For as the heavens are higher than
the earth, so are my ways higher than your ways and
my thoughts than your thoughts" (Isa. 55:9). This is
the thought which lies behind Jesus' "let it be so":
Even though our human understanding can see no
reason or purpose for this; nevertheless, let it be so
now; for thus it is *fitting* for us to fulfill all righteousness. Even though human reason cannot grasp it, this
baptism is proper, right, and fitting—it fits into God's
plan and pattern—a plan and pattern which goes
beyond the stretch of human understanding.

"Then [John] consented. And when Jesus was baptized, he went up immediately from the water, and
behold, the heavens were opened and he saw the Spirit
of God descending like a dove, and alighting on him;
and lo, a voice from heaven, saying, 'This is my beloved
Son, with whom I am well pleased.' "

In submitting to the baptism of John, Jesus lives
out and displays before our eyes a deep spiritual truth.
The truth can be expressed in three parts—

1. The Word of God does not always make sense to our human understanding.
2. We are called to obey the Word, whether we understand all the reasons behind it or not.
3. By stepping out in faith and humbly obeying the Word, we come to a deeper experience of both its truth and its power.

It is quite possible that Jesus did not fully know what was going to happen when He was baptized by John. He simply had this word from God: "Be baptized of John . . . for thus it is fitting to fulfill all righteousness." As long as Jesus stood on the bank of the Jordan River, the full truth of that word would remain shrouded in mystery. Only by stepping down into the water—only by trusting the word of God and obeying it—could Jesus experience the full truth of that word.

What mighty things hang upon obedience to the Word of God! The whole ministry of the Lord Jesus hangs in balance on the banks of the Jordan River. Without the anointing and in-filling of the Holy Spirit, there can be no ministry. But it is the will of God that this anointing and in-filling shall come by way of a baptism which, according to human reason, Jesus doesn't actually need. Thank God, He didn't get sidetracked into theological argument and speculation! Praise God, He "humbled himself and became obedient"!

In spiritual things, the pathway to understanding and truth is not by way of human knowledge and reason, but by way of obedience—humble obedience to the Word of God. Jesus lives out before our eyes this deep spiritual truth. He receives the Word of God— human reason cannot altogether grasp the necessity of it; He obeys it nevertheless—and lo! the Word of

God proves itself to be both truth and power!

As John baptized people in the River Jordan, he said that whereas he baptized with water, the One who came after him—Jesus—would baptize with the Holy Spirit. Jesus' own baptism in the Jordan River provides us with a helpful image for this baptism with the Holy Spirit, which John prophesied and which Jesus promised. In His own baptism, Jesus revealed a pattern of action whereby any Christian can enter into and experience the baptism with the Holy Spirit. This pattern moves through the three phases of truth which are portrayed in Jesus' own baptism:

1. Our human understanding cannot altogether grasp the reason or necessity for a baptism with the Holy Spirit, according to the pattern given in Scripture.
2. We are encouraged to trust and obey the Word of God nevertheless.
3. The Word of God concerning this baptism with the Holy Spirit will prove itself to be both truth and power.

From the standpoint of human reason, Jesus didn't need to be baptized: He had no sin, so why be baptized unto repentance? Likewise, for someone who is already a Christian, the baptism with the Holy Spirit has a similar 'unreasonable' aspect: "If I already have the Holy Spirit, why should I pray to receive the Holy Spirit or be baptized with the Holy Spirit? Didn't I receive the Holy Spirit when I became a Christian?"

"Of course you did."

"And that's all I need to be saved, isn't it—to believe on Christ, and have His Spirit?"

"The Bible says so, absolutely."

"Isn't the growth which I have experienced since I became a Christian—the increase of love, joy, peace, and so on—isn't this the fruit of the Holy Spirit?"

"Indeed it is!"

"Well, then, I *have* the Holy Spirit!"

"Of course you do! If you didn't have the Holy Spirit, you couldn't be a Christian. 'Anyone who does not have the Spirit of Christ does not belong to him' (Rom. 8:9)."

"All right: I'm saved and I'll go to heaven and I have the Holy Spirit. What more do I need? Isn't it just a matter of buckling down and being the kind of Christian the Lord wants me to be?"

On the day of Christ's ascension, every one of the Apostles could have made the same confession: "I believe on the Lord Jesus. I'm saved. I'm going to heaven. I have the Holy Spirit (see John 20:22)." Yet Jesus charged them "not to depart from Jerusalem, but to wait for the promise of the Father, which, he said, 'you heard from me, for John baptized with water, but before many days you shall be baptized with the Holy Spirit.' "

Beyond conversion, beyond the assurance of salvation, beyond having the Holy Spirit, there is a *baptism* with the Holy Spirit. It might not make sense to our human understanding any more than it made sense for Jesus to be baptized by John. But when John would have prevented Him, Jesus said, "Let it be so now. For thus it is *fitting* for us to *fulfill all righteousness*." There is a Divinely Appointed Pattern. It is fitting for us to fulfill it. It 'fits into' God's purpose for us. We are not called to understand it, or justify it, or explain it, but simply to enter into it in humble obedience and with expectant faith.

What is the pattern for the baptism with the Holy Spirit, as we find it in the Scripture? It is this: The Word of salvation in Christ is proclaimed; the hearer receives the word, believes, and is baptized with water;

the believer is baptized with the Holy Spirit. Sometimes the baptism with the Holy Spirit occurs spontaneously, sometimes through prayer and the laying
on of hands. Sometimes it occurs after water baptism,
sometimes before. Sometimes it occurs virtually simultaneously with conversion, sometimes after an interval
of time. So there is considerable variety within the
pattern. But one thing is constant in the Scripture, and
it is most important: It is never merely *assumed* that
a person has been baptized with the Holy Spirit. When
he has been baptized with the Holy Spirit the person
knows it. *It is a definite experience.*

This comes out clearly when Paul encounters some
disciples in Ephesus. He asks them, "Did you receive
the Holy Spirit when you believed?" The very way he
asks the question assumes that if they had received
the Holy Spirit they would know it and could give a
simple affirmative answer. In this case they had not
experienced the baptism with the Holy Spirit, so Paul
laid hands on them, and then they did experience it.

You don't have to understand or explain the baptism
with the Holy Spirit in order to experience its blessing. Jesus is our Guide: He pushed the reasonings of
John's mind gently aside, and said, "Let it be so now."
That is a word which a Christian may take for his
own in regard to the baptism with the Holy Spirit:
"Let it be so now; it is fitting!"

After Jesus had set aside the human questioning
about His being baptized, He simply stepped down into
the water. That is the second thing He shows us: Put-
ting aside all fear and doubt, you put your full trust
in the Word of God and act upon it.

This point is crucial: Jesus had to step down into
the water. He couldn't stand on the bank of the Jordan
and say, "All right, Father, I'm perfectly willing to be
baptized, if you want to baptize me. . . ." He couldn't

wait for the Jordan to flow up over its banks and immerse Him. He had to step down into the water. He had to actually *ask* for baptism, and take a step toward receiving it.

In Luke 11:5–13, Jesus makes it clear that we must *ask* for the Holy Spirit. God won't force this experience on anyone. But He is more than ready to give it to anyone who asks.

Some people say: "I just don't believe I'm *good* enough to receive this kind of blessing. I don't *deserve* it."

"Do you think *Jesus* was good enough to receive it?"

"Of course!"

"Then you have nothing to worry about. God gives this blessing on the basis of Jesus' righteousness, not yours. You accept His righteousness unto salvation— why not also for the baptism with the Holy Spirit?"

"You mean *anybody* can receive it?"

" 'The promise is to you and to your children and to all that are afar off, *every one* whom the Lord our God calls to him' (Acts 2:39). Has God called you? Are you His child through faith in Christ? (If you haven't settled that issue, it's not the time to talk about the baptism with the Holy Spirit.)"

"But I *am* His child. I *do* believe in Christ."

"Then this promise *is* for you. *'Every one* whom the Lord our God calls.' "

"But I don't want anything phoney or faked."

"No, and neither does God. Put your trust in the Word God has given you. Do you think that if you come with an honest and seeking heart, and ask the Lord to baptize you with the Holy Spirit, that He would give you a 'stone' or a 'scorpion' (Matt. 7:9)—some phoney or merely emotional experience? No, He will give you exactly what you ask for: 'How much more

will the heavenly Father give the Holy Spirit to those
who ask?' (Luke 11:13)."

There is a sound biblical theology for the baptism
with the Holy Spirit. But the baptism with the Holy
Spirit is not a theology to be discussed and analyzed:
It is an experience one enters into. A bachelor might
say some excellent and true and accurate things about
marriage. But God didn't institute marriage as an object for thought and discussion. It is a life to be lived.
If a bachelor wants to learn what marriage is really
about, he must take that walk to the altar and say,
"I do."

Will the baptism with the Holy Spirit change your
life? Will it make any real difference in your Christian
walk? Of course it will! The baptism with the Holy
Spirit is a gift of God. God does not give worthless or
no-account gifts.

A Presbyterian minister, James Brown, puts it
succinctly thus: "The disciples before Pentecost were
living behind locked doors—for fear. After they received the baptism with the Holy Spirit, they turned
the world upside down." That same transforming experience, that same dimension of power, is available
to us, for Jesus still baptizes His followers with the
Holy Spirit.

JESUS CHRIST, THE BAPTIZER

John the Baptist baptized in water. At the time of
His ascension, Jesus commanded His disciples to baptize new converts (Matt. 28:19); water baptism became
an integral part of the life of the Apostolic Church
(Acts 2:41, 8:39, 9:18, 10:47, 19:5). Through this rite
or sacrament, the Holy Spirit grafts a new believer
into the Body of Christ, the Church (I Cor. 12:13).
This baptism has two distinguishing features: It is with

water, and the one who administers the baptism is a person commissioned by the Lord to do so.

The Bible distinguishes carefully between baptism with water and baptism with the Holy Spirit. John the Baptist specifically contrasts the baptism which he gives with the baptism which Jesus will give: His is with water, Jesus' will be with the Holy Spirit. All four Gospels record this prophetic utterance of the Baptist: Matthew 3:11, Mark 1:8, Luke 3:16, John 1:31–33. Jesus observes this same distinction: "John baptized with water, but before many days you shall be baptized with the Holy Spirit" (Acts 1:5). His distinction at this point is not as to who baptizes, but rather between water baptism and Holy Spirit baptism as such. Peter applies these words of Jesus to the experience of the Gentile converts in the household of Cornelius: They received a baptism with the Holy Spirit (Acts 10:44, 11:16), after which Peter commanded that they should be baptized with water (Acts 10:47). Both during the ministry of Jesus and in the Apostolic Church, a clear distinction was maintained between baptism with water and baptism with the Holy Spirit.

Water baptism is a rite or sacrament administered by the Church, on the authority of Christ. Jesus himself never baptized with water (John 4:2). Baptism with the Holy Spirit is administered by Jesus himself. No human being has ever received the commission to baptize with the Holy Spirit. This is an office which Jesus has reserved for himself alone. He is the only baptizer with the Holy Spirit. Thus baptism with the Holy Spirit also has two distinguishing features: It is with the Holy Spirit, and the One who baptizes is Jesus himself.

Once we recognize these basic distinctions between baptism with water and baptism with the Holy Spirit, we see also the beautiful *parallel* between them. When

a person desires to be baptized with water, he presents
himself as a candidate—and the minister baptizes him.
He does not have to "do" anything. He rather allows
something to be done to him. Likewise, when a person
desires to be baptized with the Holy Spirit, he need
only present himself as a candidate—and Jesus the
Baptizer baptizes him with the Holy Spirit. He does
not have to "do" anything. He merely presents himself
to Jesus and accepts His baptism with the Holy Spirit.

*The baptism with the Holy Spirit is thus an en-
counter with Jesus Christ, the mighty Baptizer with the
Holy Spirit.* Peter made this unmistakably clear on the
Day of Pentecost when he said, "*He* has poured out
this which you see and hear" (Acts 2:33). Just as the
sinner needs an encounter with Jesus, the Lamb of
God; just as the sick one needs an encounter with Jesus,
the Healer; just as the discouraged soul needs an encounter with Jesus, the Good Shepherd—even so, the
willing but weak disciple needs an encounter with
Jesus, the Baptizer with the Holy Spirit.

We are especially indebted to Rev. David du Plessis
for this insight. In recent years the Lord has taken
him literally over the face of the whole earth. He has
challenged ministers, theologians, laymen, bishops,
seminarians, church leaders—all who would hear—to
an encounter with Jesus Christ, the Baptizer with the
Holy Spirit. The shift of emphasis from 'seeking an
experience' to 'an encounter with Christ' has opened
the door of blessing to unnumbered thousands of people.
His own explanation is given in the following letter.

Often I receive letters from folks who have
grown up in churches with a rather quiet yet
deeply reverent form of worship, where deep
emotion is appreciated, but excited emotion or
emotionalism is frowned upon. When such folks

come into churches where excited emotion is looked upon as a sign of the fullness of the Holy Spirit, they find it difficult to enjoy real worship. This particularly has reference to the 'tarrying' or 'receiving' meetings. Those who wrestle in prayer and storm the gates of heaven with great noise often end up with nothing but that, and yet feel they had a good meeting. They are the ones who complain when others are baptized in the Holy Spirit in a quiet yet deeply consecrated atmosphere. They say it was too easy. The others say the noisy wrestling, groaning, hand-wringing, falling, rolling is too emotional. Which is right?

John the Baptist declares that God said that whereas he would baptize in water, Christ would baptize in the Holy Spirit. John's baptism was a River Baptism. People could *drink* of the river, they could *splash* in the river, they could *swim* in the river, and they could *dive* in the river. All would be perfectly correct and enjoyable. But if any of these wanted to be *baptized* in the river, they would have to stop drinking, splashing, swimming, and diving. They would have to do nothing but quietly and reverently enter the water till they came to the Baptist. Before he baptized them, they would even have to stop breathing or talking. He could baptize each one only as they would stop 'doing' and allow him to immerse them. This is the image that God gave to John of the Baptism which Jesus would give.

Some drink, splash, swim, dive in order to get the Baptism in the Holy Spirit, as if it depended upon what they did. Others come quietly and in deep consecration, surrender to Christ the Baptizer, and depend on what He does for them. This is the easy Baptism. It is followed by great rejoicing. Now you can drink and splash and swim all you want to in the river of life, because it is *flowing* from within you (John 7:38). The noisy, splashing, swimming, diving approach takes longer because you have to carry on until you are exhausted by your own doings; only then can the Mighty Baptizer take you and baptize you in the Holy Spirit. The Baptism in the Holy Spirit is always easy when Jesus Christ does it for you, but always difficult when you struggle to do it yourself or with the help of others.

Those who receive the Baptism in the Holy Spirit in a noisy, excited meeting often find it almost impossible to continue to pray in the spirit when they get home. They cannot work up that excitement again, and they think that if they speak in tongues without this great excited emotion they will be doing so of themselves. Such people become disappointed and then become quiet because they feel that they themselves are working up the excitement too. That is why many never speak in tongues after they have done so the first time, under great strain and excitement.

Those who realize that *by faith* they quietly yielded to the Baptizer, and *by faith* began to speak as the Spirit gave utterance, are able to continue to do so in the quiet of their own daily devotions. Such people often experience the exciting and exhilarating power of the Spirit some time after they have received the Baptism in the Spirit and began to speak in tongues.

THE BAPTISM WITH THE HOLY SPIRIT
IN THE BOOK OF ACTS

The word 'PILOT' serves as a helpful acrostic in considering five aspects of the baptism with the Holy Spirit. Each letter in this word can represent one aspect of what the Book of Acts tells us about this experience.

P = Power

Jesus said to His disciples in Acts 1:8, "You shall receive *power* when the Holy Spirit has come upon you; and you shall be my witnesses in Jerusalem and in all Judea and Samaria and to the end of the earth." The specific promise in connection with the baptism with the Holy Spirit is the promise of power—power for witnessing.

We see a clear instance of this in Peter's sermon on the Day of Pentecost. One sermon: three thousand conversions. A group of 60 Lutheran pastors was meeting in Los Angeles to hear lectures on this subject, and after the lectures one of the pastors stood up and said, "Brethren, we need the kind of power we read about here. Peter preached one sermon and had 3000 conversions. We preach 3000 sermons and are lucky to get one convert!"

This element of power in witness is seen also in the case of St. Paul. After he had received the baptism with the Holy Spirit, it says that "immediately he proclaimed Jesus, saying, 'He is the Son of God' " (Acts 9:20). And when people raised some questions, because of his unsavory past in regard to the Christian movement, it says, "He increased all the more in strength, and confounded the Jews who lived in Damascus by proving that Jesus was the Christ."

A woman in our congregation came regularly to one of our Bible study groups. She never spoke much. But one day she began to speak and witness of Christ in a way she never had before. It had a sense of reality about it. You could tell that she wasn't 'reading it out of a book.' She was talking about Someone she knew from firsthand experience. It made a definite impression on me, but after a few days I more-or-less forgot about it. Then, a few weeks later, she was in the Sunday morning Bible class, and this same thing happened: She began witnessing in a quiet but powerful way. In the course of it, she said, "You have to have the Holy Spirit, or none of it makes any sense to you."

I felt something definite must have happened in her life, so a little while later I dropped in at her home and talked with her. She told me that, yes, something wonderful had happened to her. She was in the kitchen one day, and was quite upset about something. "Then, all at once," she said, "it was just like God came up and put His arm around my waist and I heard Him say, 'It's going to be all right.' And then, all at once, I was just full of the Holy Spirit, and I went singing into the dining room so full of joy I could hardly contain it." She went on to tell how the Lord had visited her in a similar way about three weeks later, seeming to confirm the first experience.

An interesting sidelight on our conversation was that she repeated several times: "You have to *ask* for the Holy Spirit. That's the key. You have to *ask*." It was interesting, also, that no one had spoken to her specifically about receiving the baptism with the Holy Spirit. She had simply asked . . . and received. And very shortly afterwards the experience led to outward expression in this new power to witness for Christ.

I = Instantaneous

The baptism with the Holy Spirit is an experience which happens at a definite moment in time. The Book of Acts records five instances of the baptism with the Holy Spirit: Pentecost, the converts in Samaria, Saul in Damascus, the Gentiles in Cornelius' household, and the disciples in Ephesus. In each of these cases the experience is dealt with in the *aorist* tense, which describes an action taking place at a definite point in time. Paul's question to the disciples in Ephesus, Acts 19:2, is pointedly phrased with a time-reference: "Did you receive the Holy Spirit *when you believed?*"

A person's experience of the baptism with the Holy Spirit may be quiet and unspectacular—so quiet that he may wonder at the time if he actually *had* the experience. But if it is genuine, it will begin to show in his life.

A neighboring pastor and I were together one day, and we prayed about this matter of the baptism with the Holy Spirit. There was nothing spectacular in his experience; he spoke a few sentences quietly in a new tongue. A few days later we were together for a social event, and he said, "I don't think anything actually happened." We talked about it a little, and discussed whether this experience might not be subject to attacks of doubt just as much as one's assurance of salvation. A couple of months later we were together again, and he said, "There's come about a great difference in my life and ministry—a new sense of reality. I can't pin it down to the hour and minute, but I'd say this: From 'about that time' [when he experienced the baptism with the Holy Spirit] there has been a marked change."

Some people experience a more dramatic and sudden awareness of change than this man did. But the underlying truth is the same: The experience of the baptism with the Holy Spirit is a definite event, happening at a given moment in time. There follows upon that event the process of day-by-day growth in the Spirit, but both Scripture and experience testify to the reality of this initiatory, instantaneous event where Jesus baptizes you with the Holy Spirit.

L = Link

The baptism with the Holy Spirit is a specific link in a chain of experience which unites the believer to Christ. The chain has three links: repentance and faith, water baptism, and the baptism with the Holy Spirit. Peter touches on all three on the Day of Pentecost. The people ask the disciples, "Brethren, what shall we do?" Peter answers them, "Repent and be baptized every one of you in the name of Jesus Christ for the forgiveness of your sins"—Links one and two. "And you will receive the gift of the Holy Spirit"—Link three (Acts 2:38).

The normal sequence of these links seems to be: repentance and faith, followed by water baptism, followed by the baptism with the Holy Spirit—with no significant time lapses. For all practical purposes, it is one unified experience, with three distinct aspects. This is the pattern we see in Acts 19, when Paul ministers to the Ephesian disciples: He preached to them, they believed, he baptized them, he laid hands on them and the Holy Spirit came upon them. This seems to have been the pattern on the Day of Pentecost too.

But this sequence is subject to certain variations which are important for us to notice. In the household of Cornelius (Acts 10) the sequence is inverted. The preaching of Peter, we assume, had led them to repentance and faith. But then the Lord transposed the normal sequence. Perhaps it was necessary to overcome the prejudice of the Jews, who would have been highly skeptical about a Gentile who claimed conversion. In any event, the Lord baptized them with the Holy Spirit —to the great astonishment of the Jews. But Peter sensed at once the Lord's intention, and acted to complete the chain by supplying the second link: "Can any forbid water for baptizing these people who have received the Holy Spirit just as we have?"

A woman who attended a Bible camp had an experience somewhat like the experience in Cornelius' household. She had some background and contact with the Church, but she was not baptized. In a small group meeting one evening, the Holy Spirit came upon her and she began to speak in tongues, although she had never been told about speaking in tongues, and had had no previous acquaintance with it. She was truly filled with the Spirit; she went on to interpret the tongue and then to prophesy. She had a wonderful vision of Christ. She described it to those in the group, who received a great blessing from it. When the vision passed, the first thing she said was, "When can I get baptized?"

Another significant variation in the pattern of these three links occurred in Samaria. Under the preaching of Philip, many people in Samaria came to faith and were baptized. But the third link in the chain was missing. It says in Acts 8:14–17, "When the apostles at Jerusalem heard that Samaria had received the word of God, they sent to them Peter and John, who came down and prayed for them that they might receive the Holy Spirit, *for it had not yet fallen on any of them*, but they had only been baptized in the name of the Lord Jesus. Then they laid their hands on them and they received the Holy Spirit."

This is our clearest indication in Scripture that the baptism with the Holy Spirit is an aspect of our relationship to Christ which is distinct from repentance and baptism. It is closely linked to both, but it is possible to have one without the other, as the text clearly indicates. However, *it is not considered normal to have one without the other*. That is why Peter and John went down to Samaria: to set the matter right. "Peter and John came down and prayed for them that they might receive the Holy Spirit, for it had not yet fallen on any of them."

We get the impression here that the Apostles were used to seeing the Holy Spirit simply fall upon new converts—but in Samaria it hadn't happened. So they went down *and took additional measures*—they prayed and laid on hands—and then these new converts *did* receive the Holy Spirit. The chain was complete. So here the Scripture gives us a clear example which sets apart the experience of the baptism with the Holy Spirit as a distinct aspect—a separate link—in the divinely wrought chain which binds us to Christ. And we note, further, that there *can be* a lapse of time between the forging of these separate links. The normal pattern with an adult convert is that it all happens more-or-less simultaneously, or within a brief period of time. But it can be otherwise.

Many Christian people today frankly put themselves in the place of these converts in Samaria: They have believed and been baptized, but they have no distinctive experience or conviction that they have received the baptism with the Holy Spirit. This third link in the chain is not a definite thing with them, as it was for believers in the Book of Acts. Dwight L. Moody spoke about this experience in regard to the teachers at his Bible school, and said, "Oh, why will they split hairs? Why don't they see that this is just the one thing that they themselves need? They are good teachers, they are wonderful teachers, and I am so glad to have them here, but why will they not see that the baptism with the Holy Ghost is just the one touch that they themselves need?"

A Baptist minister was talking with some friends about his ministry and said, "I've had it! I've been in the ministry twenty years, and most people would say I've been a success. But I've had it. I don't want any more new programs, new psychologies, new techniques. I want *reality!*" After a bit he relaxed in his chair, asked God to give him the baptism with the Holy Spirit, and quietly received what he asked for —just as Jesus said he would, in Luke 11:13. And no one who was with him, or who talked with him in the days and weeks following, would question that he got the reality he had longed for.

The Book of Acts thus shows us that Jesus binds us to himself by this chain of three links: repentance and faith, water baptism, and the baptism with the Holy Spirit. These three links form a perfect unity, and the believer's relationship with Christ is incomplete until all three links have been forged on the anvil of personal experience.

O = Objectivity

The experience of the baptism with the Holy Spirit is not something vague and nebulous in the Book of Acts. It is not purely subjective. It has a definite objective aspect. It is never merely assumed that a person has received the baptism with the Holy Spirit. When Jesus baptizes a person with the Holy Spirit, the person knows it. This comes out clearly when Paul encounters the disciples in Ephesus. He asks them, "Did you receive the Holy Spirit when you believed?" (Acts 19:2). The very framing of the question assumes that if they had received the Holy Spirit, they would know it, and could give a simple affirmative answer.

Another aspect of the pattern is also significant at
this point: Not only does the person *himself* know
that he has received the baptism with the Holy Spirit,
but so do those who are standing around him. Thus,
while the experience is primarily subjective, it is not
entirely so. There is some objective manifestation which
indicates to those nearby that the person has received
the baptism with the Holy Spirit.

This is clearly evident in the case of the converts
in Samaria. We are told quite matter-of-factly that
even though these people in Samaria had come to
faith and been baptized, "the Holy Spirit had not yet
fallen on any of them" (Acts 8:16). How would they
know that the Holy Spirit had not yet fallen unless
they were used to observing—and in this case had *not*
observed—some objective manifestation? When Peter
and John came down from Jerusalem and prayed with
these new converts, they *did* receive the baptism with
the Holy Spirit. And it is quite clear from the context
that this was manifested in an objective way: Simon
the Magician was so impressed by it that he tried to
buy from Peter the power to bestow the gift of the Holy
Spirit. That there was *some* kind of an objective manifestation, when these believers received the baptism
with the Holy Spirit, is thus clear.

This aspect of the pattern comes out most clearly
in Acts 10, where the outpouring of the Holy Spirit
upon the Gentiles in the household of Cornelius is
recorded. And this brings us to the last letter in our
acrostic—

T = Tongues

In Acts 10 it says that while Peter was preaching
to a group of Gentiles concerning Jesus, "the Holy
Spirit fell on those who heard the word. And the believers from among the [Jews] who came with Peter

were amazed, because the gift of the Holy Spirit had been poured out even on the Gentiles." This was now about twelve years after Pentecost, the time when Peter and all the other apostles had themselves received the baptism with the Holy Spirit. Up until then only Jews and Samaritans had become believers—not Gentiles. So the Jews who had come along with Peter were amazed, it says, because the Holy Spirit was poured out even on the Gentiles.

How did they *know* that the Holy Spirit had been poured out? The next verse tells us: "*For* they heard them speaking with tongues and extolling God." Twelve years after Pentecost, speaking in tongues was still a manifestation which believers recognized and accepted as evidence that a person had received the baptism with the Holy Spirit. For in the next chapter, when Peter reports to his Jewish friends what had happened, he says, "As I began to speak, the Holy Spirit fell on them *just as on us at the beginning.* And I remembered the word of the Lord, how he said, 'John baptized with water, but you shall be baptized with the Holy Spirit.' " Peter did not have to wonder or guess or assume that the Holy Spirit had fallen on the Gentiles. He *knew* . . . for he heard them speaking in tongues.

This, then, is the 'pilot' pattern which we find in the Book of Acts in regard to the baptism with the Holy Spirit.

Power—this is its purpose and result

Instantaneous—it occurs at a definite moment in time

Link—a distinct link in the divinely wrought chain which binds us to Christ

Objective—it has an outward manifestation

Tongues—the objective manifestation, wherever mentioned, is speaking in tongues

Is speaking in tongues the only valid objective
manifestation that a person has had this definite, instantaneous experience of the baptism with the Holy
Spirit? Scripture does not say that it is the only one.
But in showing us the pattern, Scripture gives us no
consistent suggestion of any other. In two cases in
the Book of Acts the objective manifestation is not
mentioned; in three it is, and in all of these the manifestation is speaking in tongues.

This is as far as we can go theologically. We can
discern the pattern of the baptism with the Holy Spirit
in the Book of Acts, and see the part which speaking
in tongues plays in it. But we cannot set this down as
a rigid doctrine or formula. Scripture itself shows us
that the pattern allows for considerable flexibility.

Moving from theological to practical consideration,
however, this pattern in its entirety—including speaking in tongues—can prove extremely helpful. For many
people it has been a key to a deeper walk with the
Lord, more power for serving Him, and for being an
effective witness.

We have tended to view the whole question of
speaking in tongues from a negative viewpoint: "Do
you *have* to speak in tongues when you receive the
baptism with the Holy Spirit?" Speaking from Scripture, one would have to answer, "No, there is nothing
in Scripture which says you *have* to speak in tongues."
But this is a little like a child who would ask, "Do we
have to have presents in order to celebrate my birth-
day?" We could certainly answer that child, "No, you
don't *have* to have presents on your birthday." But
it is hard to imagine many children taking delight in
that answer—or of asking the question in the first
place.

Why not look at the question of speaking in tongues from a positive viewpoint, with childlike expectancy? "You mean that if I receive the baptism with the Holy Spirit, I can also have the gift of speaking in tongues?" Again, speaking from Scripture, one could answer, "Yes, you can!" In First Corinthians, where Paul deals with the use of this gift in group meetings, we find that it becomes a specialized ministry: In a group meeting not everyone will speak in tongues. But the pattern given in the Book of Acts is for everybody. "They were *all* filled with the Holy Spirit and began to speak in tongues, as the Spirit gave them utterance." Some of the Western texts carry the intensified form *apantes*, meaning "all—every single one of them—were filled."

Many people have received the baptism with the Holy Spirit as a definite experience and reality. In their life and ministry there has been the unmistakable evidence of increased power and effectiveness. Yet they have not spoken in tongues. In the same way we could cite how God has mightily blessed and used some Christian who, let us say, has little or no acquaintance with the Epistle to the Galatians: In his study of the Scripture, he has just never settled down in Galatians. This is no proof that Galatians is unimportant, or that he himself might not receive additional power and blessing if he were to get into this Epistle. It just shows us how matchless the grace and resourcefulness of God is. He works through us despite gaps in our Christian knowledge and experience. But this does not give us license to become indifferent to these gaps—or, worse yet, to make a virtue of them. We have no way of knowing what could have been the result if some of these great men of God had also, like St. Paul, spoken in tongues.

To consummate one's experience of the baptism

with the Holy Spirit by speaking in tongues gives it an objectivity. This objectivity has a definite value for one's continued walk in the Spirit, for speaking in tongues seems to have a definite bearing on the 'pruning' and 'refining' which a Christian must go through. Could not the 'tongue of fire' on the Day of Pentecost have suggested that the 'new tongue' they were about to receive would be a 'refining fire' in their Christian experience? This is suggestive at least, in the light of John the Baptist's prophecy that Christ would baptize with the Holy Spirit *and with fire* . . . and the chaff he will burn with unquenchable fire (Matt. 3:11, 12). In any case, this is a rather common experience: Speaking in tongues seems to bring to one's awareness many areas of the life which need pruning and refining—areas one was utterly oblivious to before.

One hears deprecating remarks about 'those who need an objective sign to bolster their faith.' In many cases it no doubt has shored up a weak faith. But perhaps this is within the mercy and goodness of God: He knows that our feelings are mercurial—up one day, down the next. But regardless of feelings, that sign of the 'new tongue' is there to remind one in a special way that the Holy Spirit has taken up His dwelling in one's body.

One young housewife who has received this gift was converted in her teens. Looking back on that experience she has said, "I know now that I could have spoken in tongues at that time. . . if someone had only told me!" She believes that she was baptized with the Holy Spirit at that time, but failed to manifest the experience according to the pattern suggested in Scripture, with speaking in tongues. Consequently her spiritual growth was hampered. She says that she has experienced greater spiritual growth in the past year, since receiving the manifestation of tongues, than during the previous ten.

Here, then, is the real issue and challenge which speaking in tongues presents to our churches today. We know that our salvation does not depend upon it, for that is through the blood of Christ only. Many Christians have surely received a great measure of the Holy Spirit without the manifestation of tongues. But is there *yet a further blessing, yet a further power* which we have missed by letting this gift fall into disuse? Is God calling the Church today to fulfill the pattern which He has suggested in Scripture, to go back and re-capitulate this first step of speaking in tongues, which we have largely bypassed?

One pastor who has come into this experience characterizes it in this way: "It seems as though every gift and every blessing which I have already experienced in the Lord is *refreshed* and *re-vitalized*." One does not repudiate or deny anything which the Lord has already done in his life. *He simply opens the way for Him to do yet more!*

The central issue in the Book of Acts is not speaking in tongues, but this deeper issue of the baptism with the Holy Spirit. The disciples had walked with Jesus for three years. They themselves had ministered in great power, with miraculous signs: healings and exorcisms. They had seen and talked with Jesus after He rose from the dead. They believed in Him and loved Him and wanted to serve Him. What one of us has had a training like theirs? And yet Jesus "charged them not to depart from Jerusalem, but to wait for the promise of the Father, which, he said, 'you heard from me, for John baptized with water, but before many days you shall be baptized with the Holy Spirit' . . . you shall receive *power* when the Holy Spirit has come upon you; and you shall be my witnesses. . ."

(Acts 1:4, 8). Not until this third link had been
forged—the baptism with the Holy Spirit—did the
Lord consider His disciples prepared to become His
witnesses. If the Lord put that kind of weight upon
the baptism with the Holy Spirit, it deserves our deep-
est and most candid consideration.

In his foreword to *The Young Church in Action*,
his translation of the Book of Acts, J. B. Phillips says,
"We cannot help looking wistfully at the sheer spiritual power of the minute young Church, which was
expressed not only by healing the body, but 'by many
signs and wonders' which amply demonstrated the fact
that these men were in close touch with God."

This is why we need to gain more understanding
of this phenomenon of speaking in tongues. We must
try to learn God's purpose in setting this gift in His
Church. It is not a turning to something bizarre, out
of boredom with the present-day Church; nor a seeking after experience for experience' sake. Rather, it is
a key which God has brought back to His Church—
perhaps a very small key, but nevertheless a key—for
recapturing the power of the Young Church.

Writing further in the same vein, Phillips says,
"Of course it is easy to 'write off' this little history of
the Church's first beginnings as simply an account of
an enthusiastic but ill regulated and unorganized ado-
lescence, to be followed by a well-disciplined maturity
in which embarrassing irregularities no longer appear.
But that is surely too easy an explanation altogether.
We in the modern Church have unquestionably *lost*
something. Whether it is due to the atrophy of the
quality which the New Testament calls 'faith,' whether
it is due to a stifling churchiness, whether it is due to
our sinful complacency over the scandal of a divided
Church, or whatever the cause may be, very little of

the modern Church could bear comparison with the spiritual drive, the genuine fellowship, and the gay unconquerable courage of the Young Church."

WHAT'S IT FOR?

An Exhortation

"Brethren, it's Jesus. It's *Jesus*. The Holy Spirit comes to glorify Jesus. That's the purpose of the baptism with the Holy Spirit: to glorify Jesus.

"Everything the Holy Spirit does has one aim, and that is to magnify Jesus. What are you doing with your 'baptism'? Has it helped you glorify Jesus? That will be the ultimate proof that God has accomplished His purpose with the baptism with the Holy Spirit, when it serves to glorify Jesus."

A Testimony

"We can speak about Jesus so easily in our family, now. Our kids do, too. We could never do that before. We talked about 'church' and 'religion' and 'steward-ship' and 'commitment' . . . even 'Christ.' But not *Jesus*. That seemed—well, too personal or something. But not any more. Not since we got the baptism with the Holy Spirit. It didn't happen right away. Little by little, though, we began to feel not so embarrassed to say His Name. Like He was getting to be a Friend. Now it's just natural. He's just a part of everything we do. The whole family life revolves around Him— where He wants us to go on vacation, what He wants us to give to the Church, what He thinks about Jerry switching from paper route to football. Just everything. It's wonderful."

"You Shall Be My WITNESSES"

A SERMON

"You shall receive power when the Holy Spirit has come upon you; and you shall be my witnesses in Jerusalem, and in all Judea and Samaria and to the end of the earth" (Acts 1:8).

The Divine Summons: Called To Be a Witness

In this text we hear the last words Jesus spoke while He was still on earth. And with these words He gave His disciples a vivid picture of what He expected them to be doing until He returned. The key to these final instructions of Jesus is found in an understanding of this one phrase, "You shall be my *witnesses. . . .*"

In the church we talk a lot about 'witnessing.' (You've heard me mention it more than a little!) But how much does this phrase really mean to us? What does it mean to "be a witness"?

Where do you hear a witness in everyday life? The word is taken from the setting of a *courtroom*. A witness is someone called into a courtroom to give a testimony —to tell what he knows about the case which is being tried. This is exactly the picture or idea which lies behind the words of Jesus, "You shall be my *witnesses.*" In the last chapter of the Gospel of Luke this same scene is recorded with some additional remarks by Jesus: "You shall be my witnesses . . . and behold, I send the *promise of my Father* upon you. . . ." The "promise of the Father" is the coming of the Holy Spirit. And the name used for the Holy Spirit in Jesus' great fare-well speeches to His disciples is *Paraclete*, which we translate *Counselor*—"Counselor" in the same sense that the judge on the bench will address Perry Mason as "Counselor." He is the Counsel for the Defense. The very name used for the Holy Spirit brings this

same picture or idea before us: the setting of a courtroom trial.

You can't read very far in the Bible before you
become aware of the idea of a *legal relationship* between God and man. The setting of a trial—a court of
justice—is a deeply rooted and recurring theme in
Scripture. Throughout the Old Testament, God is portrayed as the Great Judge. "Let the assembly of the
peoples be gathered about thee; and over it take thy
seat on high: The Lord judges the peoples" (Ps. 7:7, 8).
"Vindicate me, O God, and defend my cause against
an ungodly people" (Ps. 43:1). "Let the nations be glad
and sing for joy, for thou dost judge the peoples with
equity" (Ps. 67:4). The Book of Job is thought to be
one of the oldest books in the Scripture. When Job
finds himself the victim of terrible calamities, he cries
out for a *hearing with God*: "I would speak to the
Almighty, and I desire to argue my case with God. . . .
I will defend my ways to his face" (Job 13:3, 15).

So strong was this sense of a legal relationship
between God and man in the minds of Old Testament
believers that they even felt it within their right to
demand justice of God, if justice seemed to be wanting:
"God has taken his place in the divine council; in
the midst of the gods he holds judgment: How long
will you judge unjustly and show partiality to the
wicked? Give justice to the weak and the fatherless.
Maintain the right of the afflicted and the destitute.
. . . Arise, O God, judge the earth, for to thee belong
all nations!" (Ps. 82:1, 2, 3, 8).

The promised Messiah is seen as One who renders
just judgment. "He shall not judge by what his eyes
see, or decide by what his ears hear; but with righteousness he shall judge the poor, and decide with
equity for the meek of the earth" (Isa. 11:3, 4). Looking toward the end of the age, when Jesus shall come

again, we confess every Sunday, "He shall come again to *judge* the quick and the dead."

The comparison of our relationship to God with a legal situation—a courtroom proceeding—is thus deeply rooted in Scripture. Christ draws upon it in this text because it so accurately describes what is actually taking place in the world right now, in the spiritual realm. In the spiritual realm there is a great trial going on. And in this trial Christ tells us exactly what role we are to play: We are called to be *witnesses*. We are not the judge, nor the prosecutor, nor counselor, nor policeman, nor jailer, nor spectator . . . but witness. To see this one thing clearly is to uncomplicate our Christian life immensely. It gets us out of a lot of roles God never intended us to play—and concentrates on the one thing He really wants us to do. Consider how this works out in actual experience. . .

Pre-requisite: You Must Receive the Holy Spirit

To begin with, Jesus lays down a pre-requisite to your being a witness: *You must receive the Holy Spirit.* Despite all the teaching and training which the disciples had received from Jesus, they had no real sense of mission and outreach until after Pentecost, when they had received the Holy Spirit.

This only makes sense, in the light of the courtroom picture. A witness for the defense can't take the stand until the Counselor for the Defense is also in the courtroom. For He is the One who must lay the case before the Judge; He is the One who must take the testimony of the witness and interpret and argue it to a successful verdict. A witness might have some knowledge of the case being tried, but it takes the Counselor to bring it into the courtroom, to get it on the record, and to present it to the Judge.

Last week we talked about 'receiving Christ.' We said that in Holy Baptism Christ promises to receive you. But as you grow older, there comes a time when you must receive Christ, with a conscious act of your will. That is why baptism, in the Lutheran Church, leads to Confirmation. What is true of our relationship to Christ is also true of our relationship to the Holy Spirit, for He is a Person; He is God. And the Book of Acts teaches plainly that even after the Holy Spirit has received the believer, bringing him to a saving faith in Christ, the believer must then also receive the Holy Spirit. So Jesus tells His disciples to remain in Jerusalem until they receive the Holy Spirit. That is the key—the pre-requisite—to becoming a witness for Jesus. You must receive the Holy Spirit.

Who is to receive the Holy Spirit? Every single believer! The Holy Spirit is not a special gift for a small group of privileged Christians. He is for every single believer. Every time the Holy Spirit is received, in the Book of Acts, He is received by *all*. This is God's divine pattern. Every one of you who has received Christ as your Saviour is also to receive the Holy Spirit.

How do you receive the Holy Spirit? The same way you receive salvation—by an act of faith. On the Day of Pentecost, Peter said, "Repent, and be baptized every one of you in the name of Jesus Christ for the forgiveness of your sins, and you shall receive the gift of the Holy Spirit." A gift is not something you *earn*. It is something that is given to you. The Holy Spirit is God's *gift* for every believer. He doesn't give the Holy Spirit because we have reached a certain stage of holiness or spirituality—that is a false and unscriptural teaching. You receive the Holy Spirit on the same basis that you receive salvation—as a free gift.

If a friend sends a gift to your house for your

birthday, that gift is yours. You can do with it what
you will. You can leave it on the table, all neatly pack-
aged; or you can open it up, see what it is, and put
it to use. And that is just what happens on your *new*
birth-day: When you are born again, when you become a child of God through faith in Christ, He sends
a gift to your 'house,' your body. That gift is the Holy
Spirit. At this point the Holy Spirit has received you.
He's there. He's available. You don't have to beg for
Him, you don't have to wish for Him. God has already
given Him to you. But if He is to be anything more
than a pretty package sitting on some idea-table in
your mind, you must unwrap Him, you must let Him
express himself in and through your life. That is what
it means to receive the Holy Spirit, or be baptized
with the Holy Spirit—you unwrap this gift which
Christ has given you, and let Him express himself in
and through your life.

We have had some excitement and no doubt some
misunderstanding in the congregation recently, because
the gift of the Holy Spirit has found expression among
us in what the Bible calls "speaking in tongues." What
does it mean that some of your fellow members are
practicing this in their private devotional life? It simply means that they have unwrapped a part of the
gift—a part of the gift which has been more-or-less
unused in the Church. Because it is new, we have questions about it, and this is natural. But as we let our
thinking be molded by Scripture, these questions will
be answered one by one, and we can rejoice that the
gift of the Holy Spirit is being unwrapped in our midst!

Any manifestation of the Holy Spirit, which is
according to Scripture, is cause for rejoicing in a Christian congregation. We do not believe that shouting,
dancing, yelling, rolling on the floor, and general dis-
order are a necessary part of speaking in tongues,

though this association is often made. A little boy once received a little toy tractor for Christmas. He wound it up and set it down on the living room rug. When it started to go, he got all excited. He started after it, tripped over his grandmother's foot, and spilled a cup of coffee which she had on her lap. Now this didn't mean that the tractor was a bad tractor or a dangerous toy. It just meant that the little boy had to learn to look where he was going. When we unwrap any part of the gift of the Holy Spirit, and by faith release it into our life, we have to look where we are going. We have to see in the roadmap of Scripture the purpose and 'destination' of this part of the gift.

I hope that there will be a lot of 'unwrapping' in our congregation this year. Because the Holy Spirit is Christ's gift to *every believer*. I hope that the gift of the Holy Spirit will be manifested in your lives in all the variety and power which Scripture tells us is possible. I hope that each one of you will seek with joy and expectancy to receive and manifest more of the Holy Spirit than you have right now. And I promise you, as your pastor, as God gives me grace and wisdom, that in this congregation there will be nothing encouraged or permitted which is not strictly according to the Word of God. That is our guide. When the gift of the Holy Spirit is manifested according to the Scripture it will do exactly what Christ intends it to do: It will make us more effective witnesses for Him.

This, then, is the first point in our text: The prerequisite to becoming a witness for Christ is that you receive the Holy Spirit.

The Trial Itself

Christ has called you to be a witness. This role clarifies exactly what He expects you to do—as well as some of the things He expects you *not* to do.

First of all, let's complete the cast of characters.
You are the Witness. That's your role. The Judge?
That's God. Counsel for the Defense? The Holy Spirit.
Prosecuting Attorney? Satan, the devil. He is the one
who "accuses the brethren night and day before God"
(Rev. 12:10). The Accused? The person or group
against whom Satan is pressing a charge; a person under conviction of sin, a Christian in the clutches of
temptation. (Every Christian who is a witness also
finds himself, at times, in the role of the Accused,
where he needs the Counselor and faithful witnesses
to bring him through.) This is the cast of characters.
And our purpose is to see especially what Christ expects of us, the Witness, in this proceeding.

Sometimes it is helpful to define something by
telling what it is *not*. Consider, therefore, some of the
things your role as witness does *not* include. It does
not include the job of convincing. That is the job
of the Counselor, the Holy Spirit. A lot of witnessing
misses the mark because a Christian thinks that he
has to argue the other person into believing what he
himself has found to be true. But this is not your job.
This is the job of the Holy Spirit. When you have
made your honest witness to the truth, He will begin
to lay it to that person's heart in a way far more convincing than you could ever do. There's a time for a
witness to take the stand and give his testimony. When
that time comes, Christ expects you to speak up and
tell what you know. But there is also a time to step
down from the stand and let the Counselor take over
the job of arguing the case through to a successful
verdict.

Secondly, you are not the Prosecutor. You are not
called in to condemn someone else and point out all
his sins. True enough, when you are on the witness

stand, and Satan points out certain sins, you have to admit that they are true and that they are contrary to the law of God. This you must say, for you are sworn to tell the whole truth. But wait—you get to return to the stand when the Counselor calls for cross-examination!

"You know the Accused?"

"Yes, I know him."

"You have heard the accusations against him—violation of the law of God?"

"Yes, I have heard the accusations."

"You know them to be true?"

"Yes, they are true."

"Now, do you know, from your own knowledge and experience, whether there is any way for the Accused to avoid the penalty this involves?"

"Objection! It is irrelevant for the Accused to hear the penalty for—"

"Objection overruled! The Accused has every right to know exactly what is at stake—his life."

"Now, once again, do you know, from your own knowledge and experience, of any way for the Accused to avoid the penalty of death?"

"Yes, there is a way."

"What is the way? Speak plainly, so the Accused may hear every word."

"He must find Someone to take the penalty for him."

"Objection! The Accused must pay for his own crime."

"Your Honor, the Law of Substitution is a clearly stipulated Divine Ordinance. We are prepared to cite precedents from earliest times."

"Objection overruled."

"I repeat my last question: What must the Accused do to avoid death?"

"He must find Someone to take the penalty for him."

"And Who is that?"

"The Lord, Jesus Christ."

"How is He able to take the penalty?"

"He already *has* taken it. through the shedding of His blood."

"Objection! The Accused has done nothing to mer-it—"

"Objection overruled. The blood of Christ is a free gift to anyone who asks for it."

Now Satan will begin his parade of false witnesses, trying to convince the Accused that Christ really *won't* take the penalty, that His blood has no real power to wipe out sin, that this promise of salvation is all a sham, that the Counselor is exaggerating the penalty, and so on. You may be recalled as a witness, to shed further light on the case. But your overriding concern is always merely to give a good testimony *for Christ* ... to speak clearly of Christ's forgiving power ... not to aid Satan in condemning the Accused.

How easy it is for us to play right into Satan's hands by agreeing with Satan's condemnation—and then jumping down off the witness stand before the Counselor has a chance to present the case for Christ which would *remove* the condemnation. "For there is *no* condemnation to those who are in Christ Jesus" (Rom. 8:1).

A third thing: You are not the Judge. This points up, especially, our relationship with other Christians. When the Counselor has persuaded the Accused of Christ's forgiveness—and he has accepted it—the Judge pronounces him acquitted. The Judge, at this point, through the Counselor, will give the Acquitted some practical, Fatherly advice on what to do with his new-found freedom. This will vary according to the person

involved. The advice He gave you may differ from
the advice He gives someone else, because you are
different people, with different needs and potentials.

In a Christian congregation, we need to guard
against the temptation of edging up into the Judge's
bench. We cannot order and direct everyone else's
life according to the pattern of our own—even when
that has been given us by God. "I've found it helpful
to pray every morning from 6:00 to 7:00—so everyone
else should too! I understand a particular Christian
truth in a particular way—so everyone else should too!
I've eliminated this or that from my life—so everyone
else should too!" No, we are not the Judge.

When an issue comes up between Christians, we
can each one of us give our testimony—that is what
we are called to do. When all of the witnesses have
been heard, we are called each one to listen to the
persuasions of the Counselor. We let the Holy Spirit
speak to us and show us what is really at stake, and
what decision we ought to make.

For a Christian, this is one of the most blessed truths
we can know. Our call is to tell the truth whenever
we have the opportunity. And with our life as well as
our words! For a testimony can be made as much by
what we are as by what we say. Indeed, if what we say
is not backed up by what we are, our testimony is liable
to be thrown out of court as unreliable.

Yes, a *blessed* truth! For it outlines so clearly our
relationship to other people who are under Satan's condemnation. We have a testimony which can set them
free. We are not a policeman with a club nor a
prosecutor with a charge—but a witness with a testimony of hope. And we are not in this alone: We are
not called upon to stand up against the Master Deceiver,
the Master Accuser, with our own mere words. We
have a Counselor who can take our simple testimony,

and argue it before the court with such skill and power that He will outdo every lying, cheating trick of Satan, until the Judge of heaven and earth gavels out the verdict: "Not guilty! The Accused has pled the blood of Christ. He is commended to the fellowship of the Lord's people!"

Post-Trial Commentary

Surely Jesus could have appointed angels and archangels to be His witnesses, for they also know the truth, and could bear testimony to it. But He must have known that simple, erring, and basically frightened human beings would listen more readily to the testimony of a fellow human than to some angelic personage.

"Here is someone who knows how I feel, how I think, how I have to live my life. Of course an angel could experience the reality of God. But here is someone just like me, who claims to have experienced it. If *he* has experienced the reality and presence of Jesus, maybe *I* can too."

Yes, it is our testimony—our weak and ignorant and fallible human testimony—on which Jesus rests His case. When the Divine Summons comes, may we be ready!

3

speaking in tongues as 'gift'

The Significance of Speaking in Tongues for the Life of the Individual Believer, as He lives and Serves Within the Congregation

Suppose you were at a convention of automotive engineers. A man gives a series of lectures on the purpose and functioning of spark plugs. You certainly would not conclude that the only thing needed for transportation nowadays is a spark plug; if you want to get from one place to another, just straddle a spark plug and take off!

Spending several hours learning about spark plugs wouldn't mean that you forget about the rest of the car, nor that you give undue emphasis to the spark plugs. It just means that you are trying to come to a clearer understanding of the purpose and functioning of spark plugs—so that this part of the car—along with every other part—will contribute to maximum performance when you take off on a trip.

So it is with our consideration of speaking in tongues. We don't want to emphasize it out of proportion to its significance, nor isolate it as a self-centered phenomenon. We want to consider the purpose of this gift of the Holy Spirit, in order that it can function within the Body of Christ as God intends it to.

People often ask, "What value does speaking in tongues have?" The first and most fundamental answer to that question is given in I Corinthians 12:28,

"*God has appointed* in the church first apostles, second prophets, third teachers, then workers of miracles, then healers, helpers, administrators, *speakers in various kinds of tongues.*" If this were the only text in Scripture which mentioned speaking in tongues, we would have to conclude that it has value, *for God himself has appointed it.* Certainly God would not appoint for His Church anything worthless, harmful, foolish, silly, or inconsequential. Our whole doctrine of God— and especially of His wisdom—would be thrown into jeopardy if we were to question seriously the value of speaking in tongues as such. The single fact that it is *God* who has appointed it is *prima facie* evidence that it must have value. Our task is neither to establish nor discredit the value of speaking in tongues, but merely to discover the value which God has already placed upon it.

In the previous chapter we considered speaking in tongues as it relates to the experience of the baptism with the Holy Spirit. In the following chapter we will be looking at this gift as it relates to and functions within the Body of Christ, as one of various 'ministries' in the Church. In this chapter we look more closely at speaking in tongues as such, and see what the Bible says about the nature and purpose of this gift.

VALUE AND BLESSING

Speaking in tongues brings to one's private devotions the special blessing of 'praying in the spirit' as distinct from praying with the understanding. This comes out in I Corinthians 14:2, 14, and 28: "One who speaks in a tongue speaks not to men but to God. . . . If I pray in a tongue, my spirit prays but my mind is unfruitful. . . . If there is no one to interpret, let each of them keep silence in church and speak to himself and to

God." These verses tell us two things about speaking in tongues. First, the direction is 'upward,' a speaking unto God; it is prayer. And secondly, the mind is 'unfruitful'; the prayer is not shaped by the intellect, but by the spirit.

One immediately wonders, "What possible value can speaking in tongues have, if I have no idea what I am saying?" According to the Bible, even though you do not understand what you are saying, your spirit is in a state of prayer (I Cor. 14:14). But it is a praying with the spirit rather than the mind. It is neither an emotional nor intellectual act (although both emotion and intellect may be affected), but *an act of spiritual worship.*

It would seem that prayer in which the mind is unfruitful would have little value. What blessing can it be to pray when you have no idea what you are praying about? Actually, this is one of its greatest blessings —the fact that it is not subject to the limitations of your human intellect. The human mind, wonderful as it is from the hand of the Creator, has limited knowledge, limited linguistic ability, limited understanding, and furthermore is inhibited with all manner of prejudice, little and large. Speaking in tongues is a God-appointed manner of praying which can bypass the limitations of the intellect. One may picture the difference something like this: A prayer with the mind comes upward from the heart, and must then pass through a maize of linguistic, theological, rational, emotional, and personal check-points before it is released upward. By the time it 'gets out,' it may be little more than a slender trickle. An utterance in tongues comes upward from the depths, but instead of being channeled through the mind, it bypasses the mind and flows directly to God in a stream of Spirit-prompted prayer, praise, and thanksgiving.

A man came in one day and talked about this
whole matter of praying in the Spirit, and after a
while we went to the altar and prayed about it together. After a little while he began praying quite
fluently in tongues. He stayed there at the altar by
himself for some time, quietly worshipping in this
new way. Afterward he told me that he had never
been able to pray out loud before, not even in his
private devotions. He was of Greek Orthodox background, a man without much formal education, and
the most he had ever done before was to cross himself
and say the Name of Jesus. "Now," he said, "I can
pray as long as I want to, and it just keeps coming."

This touches on the truth which St. Paul writes
about in Romans 8:26, 27: "We do not know how to
pray as we ought, but the Spirit himself intercedes
for us with sighs too deep for words. And he who
searches the hearts of men knows what is the mind
of the Spirit, because the Spirit intercedes for the saints
according to the will of God." When the mind reaches
that point of 'not knowing how to pray as we ought,'
one may pray in the Spirit, trusting that the right
prayer—the necessary prayer at that moment—is being offered.

Another blessing in this kind of prayer is that you
are able to do it at times and in situations where normal
prayer, requiring the concentration of the mind, would
be impossible. A woman who worked in a garment factory told her pastor that she came out of work every
night feeling inwardly polluted, because of all the foul
talk which she heard around her all day long. The
pastor told her to try praying silently in tongues as
she did her work, which she could easily do, since
praying in this way leaves the mind free to concentrate
on routine tasks. She did this, and said that it was like
an invisible shield had been put up around her, screen-

ing out all the foul talk. She came out of work at the end of the day feeling spiritually refreshed and invigorated. Praying in tongues may be one way to help us "pray without ceasing," according to St. Paul's exhortation (I Thess. 5:17).

"He who speaks in a tongue edifies [builds up] *himself"* (I Cor. 14:4). This is another distinct blessing which the Bible tells us is conveyed through this gift. A woman who experienced this blessing wrote the following letter to her former pastor:

> During the past year my husband and I have felt a deepening in our spiritual lives. . . . We found ourselves searching for the truth of God and His will for us. I prayed that He would reveal His presence and give me a closer walk with Christ and fill me with the Holy Spirit. In January this year, God started answering this prayer, but not in the way I would have expected. It has worked out almost in steps which I can see now that a few months have passed by. First, He gave me a real sense of His presence but with it came this strange gift of spiritual speaking. Believe me, it was a very humbling experience. After all, I'm a college graduate and have always been grateful that I was given a good mind and a keen intellect. Instead of giving me great wisdom or understanding, which I felt I was capable of, He gave me this seemingly useless language. How could a language be useful if nobody understands it? Yet, I knew of others who had received this, and were rejoicing about it.
>
> Our pastor explained to me that its purpose in each individual seems to be somewhat different, but in general it is most useful in one's

private devotions. He encouraged me to use it
in that way and to wait and see what purpose
the Lord had in giving it to me.

As the weeks went on I tried to follow this
suggestion, but I became discouraged. This
strange language was doing nothing for me. But
gradually I became aware that my thoughts
were shifting from myself and my daily activities to God and His greatness and His love for
man. My everyday activities were truly being
done to His service and the presence of Christ
was closer to me every day. I have always tried
to live my life as a service to God and to be
close to Christ, but it was an effort. Now it
comes naturally, almost without effort. Now it
seems that God is doing these things for me. I
can take no credit whatever for this change.
All the glory must be to God.

Here is a person speaking spontaneously out of
her own experience, without any attempt at theological
reflection, and yet she pinpoints accurately the meaning of this verse, "He who speaks in a tongue edifies
himself." We are accustomed to think of edification in
purely intellectual terms. But Paul says specifically
that when you pray in tongues your mind is "unfruitful." When you exercise this gift in your private devotions, some other part of you, besides the intellect, is
being built up. (In the private use of the gift, interpretation is not necessary, I Cor. 14:28.) The edification
spoken of in this verse thus has the total person in view.

It might be well to say a word about some of the
'testimonies' people give after experiencing this gift.
"Oh! Suddenly I was just overflowing with love and
peace and joy—all the fruits of the Spirit blossomed
in an hour .... The Word of God almost jumped off

the page at me, with new meaning and power. . . . I can witness with such ease. . . . Even family and business affairs have undergone near-miraculous changes!"

People who give these testimonies are sincere, but they perhaps give way to the human tendency to exaggerate. They may have heard the testimonies of other people and unconsciously framed their own testimony after that pattern, rather than telling simply and accurately what has actually happened. They may even try to force or imagine a certain result, thinking that they have not received the full blessing if they don't get exactly what Mr. So-and-so got. This kind of testimony can be misleading and even quite discouraging to those who look honestly at themselves, and see few of these 'immediate' results in their own life and experience.

When you get closer to people who have had this experience, and watch them over a longer period of time, you actually discover great *variety* in their experiences. Perhaps the working of the gift is something like this: As a person prays in tongues, he is edified—built up—in that part of his life where he most needs building up. This would seem consistent with the working of the Holy Spirit, for He always deals with us as individuals.

Imagine, for instance, a person who has lived with a nagging doubt as to the certainty of her salvation. She knows all the Scripture promises. She has laid hold on them as best she could. Yet the freedom to say, "I am a child of God" with bell-ringing certainty has not been hers. A young housewife testified in this vein—

> I was asked recently, "Just what has speaking in tongues done for you?" What has helped me the most is that even though I have been a Christian all my life, and have attended church

regularly since I was a child, I have never been
sure I was forgiven my sins and would be
acceptable to Christ. For many years this has
been a secret worry, only spoken of to my pastor
and most intimate friends. Now I have the assurance that the Lord is with me, guiding me,
comforting me in times of need. I know now that
Jesus loves me. I know this because I now have
a personal relationship with Him.

This is the experience of one person. The Lord used
this gift first of all to build up her assurance of salvation. Since then He has moved into other areas of
her life.

Elsewhere in a congregation, you may find a person whose experience follows an altogether different
pattern. A deacon in one congregation said: "Speaking
in tongues for me has become a daily worship and like
the rest of the worship of the Lord, I would be lost
without it. Since I received this gift, the Holy Spirit
has taken away some habits that would have been hard
to do by myself, such as smoking cigarettes." This man
works as a foreman in a can factory. One evening, after
work, he lit up a cigarette. "All at once," he tells, "that
cigarette tasted so lousy it made me sick. I thought it
was because I had a big cold in my head. I spit it out
of my mouth—and I haven't touched one since. I tell
you, the Lord just took that habit out of me by the
roots. Man, when the Lord cleans you out, He really
cleans you out good!"

The striking feature in this man's testimony is that
he does not talk about struggle or willpower. He just
gives God the credit for taking the habit away from
him.

These two examples merely illustrate the point
that the edification which one experiences through the

exercise of speaking in tongues is on a highly individual basis. Your own program of sanctification is tailormade by the Holy Spirit according to your individual need, and according to the place He is preparing you for in the Body of Christ. Of course this is true in a general way, whether a person speaks in tongues or not. The intellect, however, has an inveterate tendency to categorize and legalize. When the intellect steps aside, the Spirit can operate through this gift with a freer hand, building us up not where we may think we need building up, nor where someone else thinks we need it, but where He, in divine wisdom, *knows* that we need building up. Exactly how or why it happens is difficult to explain, but both Scripture and experience bear out this truth: *Through this simple, yet supernatural and God-appointed way of praying, one's life in Christ is wonderfully built up.*

Speaking in tongues offers a new dimension in the worship of God. "One who speaks in a tongue speaks not to men but to God . . . he utters mysteries in the Spirit" (I Cor. 14:2, 3). "They heard them speaking in tongues and *extolling God*" (Acts 10:46).

Even though a person who speaks in tongues doesn't understand with the mind what he is saying, he does have a clear sense of communion with God. One person has put it this way: "When I pray in English, I sometimes have to go on for quite a time before I seem to 'make contact.' In tongues I make contact almost at once, and the sense of the Presence is more real." This, of course, is a highly subjective statement. Not everyone who speaks in tongues could say the same thing, and some who do not speak in tongues *could* witness to a similar sense of God's presence as they pray in English, or just meditate silently. Yet it is quite generally true that the sense of communion with God, and greater freedom to express one's praise and adoration, is rather common with the exercise of this gift.

A woman in our congregation had a painful back ailment, and we had been praying for her healing. As we continued in prayer, it became evident to all of us, and to the woman herself, that God intended to perform this healing through surgery. So she made arrangements and went in for surgery. She was in convalescence for about seven weeks. During this time she read her Bible and prayed a great deal. One day she tells that she had this deep-down desire to "live her life for Jesus twenty-four hours a day." And then she found herself speaking in a language which she had never learned. (She was European-born, and knows about seven languages.) She didn't know precisely what it was, because no one had told her about speaking in tongues. She described it this way in her own testimony:

> The words came as fluently as if it had been my native language. I felt a closeness to God that I had never before experienced. Although this was a surprise to me, I did not try to analyze this miracle, but accepted it as a gift from God which I needed for a more perfect communion with Him. At the time I received this gift I did not know anything about 'speaking in tongues.' A week later, however, a friend of mine read me a magazine article which left me eager to know of other's experience similar to mine.

This new dimension in one's private worship and communion with God is surely one of the greatest blessings of speaking in tongues. It can take a variety of forms. One may "sing in the spirit," as St. Paul says, the words and melody forming together spontaneously, which can be a wonderful outpouring of the soul unto God in praise and adoration. The mood of the praying will vary from time to time, suggesting that one expresses a variety of prayers in tongues just as in English, such as praise, adoration, thanksgiving, confession, intercession, petition, and so on.

One person became a little disturbed because he felt so burdened, almost depressed, one time as he was praying in tongues. Then it came to him that this was a prayer of confession, and as he continued praying, the burden lightened. Another person mentioned a similar experience, except that it seemed to be a burden of intercession. Perhaps these are the "sighs too deep for words" which St. Paul speaks about in Romans 8—things out of the reach of the understanding, things which the Spirit searches out in the heart of man and in the heart of God, and deals with through this supernatural gift.

Enhancement of one's private worship is the essential blessing of speaking in tongues. The other blessings are summed up in it: *As you worship God in tongues, your mind is at rest and your spirit prays, unhindered by the limitations of the human understanding, and through this act of worship the Holy Spirit builds up your life in Christ.*

QUESTIONS AND PROBLEMS

No gift of the Holy Spirit is so freighted with doubts, misgivings, questions, and misunderstandings as speaking in tongues. We want to consider these questions honestly and objectively, under the heading of three words which loom large wherever speaking in tongues comes up for discussion: Emotionalism. Over-emphasis. Divisiveness.

Emotionalism

"Doesn't speaking in tongues open the door to a lot of uncontrolled emotionalism? In churches with a dignified and restrained worship tradition—such as Episcopalian, Lutheran, Presbyterian, Catholic—this question can give rise to real disturbance, both for the individual Christian and for the congregation.

One man told how his mother had belonged to a church where speaking in tongues was practiced. As a child he was taken to meetings in the church. He saw people shaking, screaming, actually rolling on the floor —often in connection with speaking in tongues. Memories like this are hard to erase. This man, as he grew up, turned adamantly against this whole manner of religious expression, and vowed to have nothing more to do with it. In spite of this considerable and well-grounded prejudice, however, he later came to the conviction that God wanted him to have the gift of speaking in tongues. He prayed and received it. But when he spoke in tongues, it was calm and unemotional—just a quiet speaking, with an undertone of joy. His witness as to what this has meant in his life and ministry has the same note of quiet restraint, and yet it has become precious and real in his own life.

The manner in which a person expresses the gift of tongues is not determined primarily by the gift itself. It is largely determined by the individual himself, and by the religious setting. If a man worships in a religious setting where the emotions are expressed in a loud and exuberant fashion, and if he himself is similarly inclined, then he will likely express speaking in tongues in this way. (He would also put the same feeling into singing "The Old Rugged Cross.") But if he has grown up in a religious setting where the quieter emotions of awe and reverence have been cultivated, he is most likely to speak in tongues in this same reserved way.

In a prayer group of Lutherans and Episcopalians, for example, the speaking in tongues will be no more pronounced in its emotional aspect than prayers in English. The reason speaking in tongues is tied to emotionalism in many people's minds is because the practice of it, until quite recently, has been confined almost exclusively to religious groups which follow a rather free and emotional form of worship.

Perhaps a further reason for this misconception is that the only mention of speaking in tongues in the Scripture, outside of the Book of Acts and the last chapter of Mark's Gospel, is the letter to the Church at Corinth. In this congregation, lack of inhibition seemed to be the order of the day. Nor was this limited to the exercise of speaking in tongues. In the eleventh chapter, we read that they were getting drunk at Holy Communion. Here, again, it was not the gift which led to emotionalism, but rather, the gift was being used in a setting where people were already disposed toward this kind of expression.

A third reason for this misconception lies in the frequent use of the term "ecstatic utterance" as a synonym for speaking in tongues. As we have already seen, there is no warrant in Scripture for the use of this as a term to describe speaking in tongues. It is always referred to simply as a 'speaking.' The Greek word *ekstasis*, the root of our English "ecstasy," is never used to describe a speaker in tongues. On two occasions in the Book of Acts, this word is used to describe those who *hear* someone speak in tongues, and is usually translated "amazed." The idea that a speaker in tongues goes off into a kind of religious ecstasy, where he loses emotional and personal control, is contrary both to Scripture and actual experience. The person who exer-

cises this gift is perfectly able to remain in full control
of himself and his emotions. If he weren't, St. Paul
would not be able to give such direct and down-to-earth
instruction as he does in I Corinthians 14:28, "If there
is no one to interpret, let the speaker in tongues keep
silence in church and speak to himself and to God."

Overemphasis

"Isn't speaking in tongues overemphasized whenever it comes on the scene?"

This is often the case. It can be and has been
overemphasized. The reason for this overemphasis seems
to be twofold.

The first reason is readily understandable. Speaking
in tongues can be a deeply moving personal experience,
opening up new spiritual horizons. Any person who
has this kind of experience is eager to share it with
others. For a time he may overdo it. We see this same
kind of thing in people who are newly converted. A
man was converted while he was in the Navy, and
he came home all fired up to convert his family and
friends. The wife said, a little wryly, "I'll have to
admit, we did lose most of our friends that first year."
In the first flush of experience, speaking in tongues
may come to have a disproportionate emphasis in a
congregation, or in the personal life and witness of
an individual.

The answer to this kind of thing is wise and understanding pastoral guidance. First of all, a pastor or
friend should honestly *rejoice* in the person's experience
(I Cor. 12:26). At the same time, it must be pointed
out that this is only one aspect of the Faith. It should
not become the focal point of one's life or witness.
Indeed, it is often wise to keep one's experience of
speaking in tongues as a "holy secret" for a time, until

it has a chance to root down in one's life. Talking about spiritual experiences too freely can be detrimental to one's continued growth. Furthermore, one needs to live with this experience, as with any experience, for some time before he is able to give a balanced impression of it to someone else. To share it with a wise and understanding friend, however, is not only right but probably necessary. Such a friend, ideally the person's own pastor, can share the joy, and then also offer the kind of counsel which will help knit this experience into the total fabric of one's Christian life.

When people receive this kind of pastoral care, they do not give speaking in tongues undue emphasis in their testimony or conversation. They are more likely to talk about the Lord, or about some new discovery in the Bible, than about speaking in tongues.

A second reason for overemphasis is more difficult to deal with. Sometimes real antagonism rises up toward speaking in tongues as such, or towards those who advocate it. This no doubt springs from a variety of causes, but when it is present, it leads to a kind of negative overemphasis of the gift. The gift is constantly pushed into the spotlight by argument and debate *against* it. This will more than likely evoke a defensive reaction on the part of those who believe in the gift.

Suppose a man came to work in a factory where all of the employees had only four fingers on each hand—the little finger was missing. The other employees soon notice that he has a little finger. At first it evokes some curiosity, but before long also some antagonism.

"You don't need to think you're any better than we are, just because you have a little finger."

"Well, I don't but I like it—"

"We've gotten along without little fingers in this factory for a long time!"

The man shrugs and lets the matter drop. But every time he's on a lunch or coffee break, someone begins to question or challenge him about this little finger.

"We can work the machines with our four fingers just as well as you can. What good is that little finger anyway?"

"Well, it's the way God made me, and I find it helpful."

"It's causing all sorts of argument and trouble in the plant. Why don't you cut it off and be like the rest of us?"

"No, I don't want to. It's part of my body. I like my little finger."

This little finger is tremendously overemphasized as to its real importance *because it is constantly being challenged.* The overemphasis comes not because of the *use* of the little finger, but because of its mere *presence.*

This kind of overemphasis often occurs in connection with speaking in tongues. People who may never even have heard a person speak in tongues stir up much argument and discussion concerning it. Even when those who speak in tongues would be happy to let the matter rest, it is continually brought up to be challenged and questioned. When someone has received a blessing from God, and then has that blessing challenged as though it were something low and almost shameful, he will naturally speak out to defend that blessing.

The perfect answer to this situation is given in I Corinthians 12:26: "If one member is honored, all rejoice together." Gordon Bordine, a Lutheran pastor who had not experienced speaking in tongues, expressed this basic attitude in a letter to the writer:

> Much thought and prayer have been given to this matter of speaking in tongues. I have not

had the experience, but I feel God is leading in other areas of my ministry. I still look with expectancy toward this gift—*if not for myself at least for some of the members of the congregation.*

If other members of the congregation can *honestly rejoice* with those who receive this gift, a lot of overemphasis will be put quietly to rest. If those who speak in tongues find themselves in a welcome and understanding environment, their own tendency toward overemphasis can be dealt with more effectively.

Divisiveness

"Why does speaking in tongues so often result in divisiveness?" Denominations, congregations, even families, get split up over it. What's behind it?

In his book, *Tongue Speaking*, Morton Kelsey quotes K. G. Egertson, a Lutheran pastor, who says: "The cause of divisiveness is either that those 'for' or 'against' become militant." This is an incisive insight into the real cause for divisiveness: It is not speaking in tongues that is divisive. (We surely cannot attribute divisiveness to a gift from the Holy Spirit! He would hardly inject a divisive element into the Church which He is sanctifying!) The cause of divisiveness is always to be found in the ignorance and sinfulness of man, coupled with the agitation and devices of Satan.

If an objective observer were to enter a situation where divisiveness had occurred over speaking in tongues, he would likely find two dynamics at work, in varying proportions, depending upon the particular situation:

1. Lack of wisdom, decency, and order in the use of the gift, or in conversation and witnessing concerning it.

2. A rejection or suppression of the gift in the congregation.

Scripture warns against both of these extremes. Turning to the left, St. Paul says, "Let all things be done decently and in order" (I Cor. 14:40). Turning to the right he says, "Quench not the Spirit; despise not prophesying; forbid not speaking in tongues" (I Thess. 5:19, 20; I Cor. 14:39).

In 1962 The American Lutheran Church appointed a Study Commission to look into the practice of speaking in tongues in its member congregations. In its official report, the committee called attention to these two factors:

> It is possible to have unity with diversity if Christ is Lord and His love reigns over all. The respect of members of one group for those of the other is occasionally expressed, but a statement such as "speaking in tongues is not Lutheran," does not make for a better spirit in the congregation, nor does the "If-you-don't-like it-lump-it" attitude.

If people involved in a situation of divisiveness— especially church officials, pastors, and lay leaders of a congregation—see clearly these two dynamics, they will have gone a long way toward bringing about a spirit of love and harmony. They will speak a word of admonition to those who *have* experienced the gift, and a word to those who have *not*. When the responsibilities of each are clearly drawn out, and accepted, the conditions for peace and harmony are present.

George Aus, professor of Dogmatics at Luther Theological Seminary, St. Paul, Minnesota, wrote just this kind of advice to our congregation when we were wrestling with this question:

> To those who *have* experienced the gift: 1) Be
> sure that the purpose for which you use it is
> positive, i.e., for edification—whether private or
> corporate. 2) Let the Spirit sift your motives in
> the public use of the gift. 3) One of the risks in
> this gift is that it can become divisive. Be in
> prayer that if it becomes divisive it be not due
> to you—or your use of the gift, e.g., when it is
> used to exalt self in the display of spiritual
> excellence. 4) Beware of spiritual pride.
>
> To those who have *not* experienced the gift:
> 1) If the exercise of the gift by others edifies
> you—thank God. 2) Do not be disturbed by the
> fact that it has not been given to you. This fact
> does not mean that something is wrong with you
> or that you are an inferior or carnal Christian.
> 3) Your function in the edification of the con-
> gregation may call for other gifts. What kind of
> a body would it be if everyone were a foot?

We have seen this kind of advice work out within a single family. The wife had experienced the gift, the husband had not. She was happy in her experience, and grew marvelously as a result of it, but she did not overplay it. He, on the other hand, genuinely rejoiced with her, even though he himself had not received the gift. He also grew spiritually in a wonderful way. Harmony on this basis is no theory, but a definite possibility and reality.

If those who speak in tongues are modest and orderly, and if those who do not speak in tongues accept the presence of the gift in the congregation, and rejoice with those who have received it, the congregation will be knit together in peace and harmony.

Pastoral Guidance

The pastor is usually the key to how speaking in tongues will be received and used in the Church. Whether a pastor himself experiences the gift is a matter between him and the Lord. But that he will need to give sound pastoral guidance in the matter is a virtual certainty. This movement of the Holy Spirit is now becoming widespread. Undoubtedly there is much in it which is of the flesh, or in which wisdom has been lacking. But it is real, and our people are coming into this experience in increasing numbers. The question is no longer, "Should we have this experience?" Our people are going to have it: In a prayer group, through listening to the testimony of a neighbor who has come into the experience, through reading about it—in one way or another—our people are receiving this experience. They need good pastoral guidance. There can be a lot of poor theology and a lot of undisciplined practice tied to a perfectly genuine experience. God expects the pastor to shepherd his people in this matter just as he would in any other matter of the Faith.

One young girl received this gift of speaking in tongues, and her first thought was, "Oh, I must tell my pastor!" She was all enthused, as only a teen-ager can be, and expected her pastor to share this joy. He remarked coldly, "Well, I don't suppose we can expel you from the church for this, but—" The impression he left was that she had done something almost serious enough to warrant expulsion from the church. This is tragic. The Bible tells us to "try the spirits"—not condemn them out of hand, on blind prejudice. The pastor who downgrades the experience of speaking in tongues, to a parishioner who has experienced the gift, misses a great opportunity to lead this person on in the things of God.

The Lord put the gift of tongues in His Church for a specific purpose. If He is bringing this gift back into the Church in these days, surely the pastors of the Church will be held accountable for the way in which it is received and used—whether to spread doubt and dissension, or to glorify God.

Members of our congregation have lived with this experience now for a number of years. It has brought many blessings to our people, and has also presented certain problems. The following summary of the theological and practical aspects of speaking in tongues has been helpful as we have sought to integrate this experience into the on-going life and witness of our congregation.

I. Theological Aspects

A. Historic Doctrine

1. *No specific doctrine has been formulated.* So far as we know, the basic catholic and Reformation Confessions contain no definite statement about speaking in tongues. Here we can remind our people that these Confessions concern themselves with the central doctrines of the Christian Faith, relating especially to Faith and Salvation. Speaking in tongues is a minor aspect of faith and practice on which the churches have had no occasion to speak or to formulate any specific doctrine.

2. *The doctrine, however, is implicit in Scripture.* All true doctrine is based on the Bible. The historic Christian denominations accept the Bible as the revealed Word of God. (The historic Confessions are simply an accurate explanation or application of the central truths of the biblical revelation.) Therefore, since speaking

in tongues is clearly spoken about in the Bible, Christian people can be assured that this is not a 'new teaching': Everything the Bible says about speaking in tongues has always been an implicit part of Christian doctrine.

3. *The experience, not the doctrine, is "new."* What we are encountering in our day is not a new doctrine, but the *experience* and *practice* of a doctrine which we have always implicitly held. We have always believed in speaking in tongues, as a part of the biblical revelation, but our people have not widely experienced speaking in tongues.

Our concern, now, is that the present-day practice of speaking in tongues conform to what God has revealed in the Bible. The task we face is to make explicit what up until now has been implicit, to explain clearly what the Bible says about speaking in tongues, and to apply it to the personal and corporate life of our people.

B. Biblical Teaching

1. *Speaking in tongues is a gift of the Holy Spirit.* The Bible says that speaking in tongues is a manifestation or gift of the Holy Spirit (Acts 2:4; 10:46; 19:6; I Cor. 12:10). Jesus spoke of it as a "sign" which would follow those who believe in Him (Mark 16:17). After Jesus' ascension it appeared as an evidence or sign that a person had been filled or baptized with the Holy Spirit (Acts 2:4; 10:46; 11:16; 19:6). Paul describes it as one of the nine *charismata* or "gifts" of the Holy Spirit (I Cor. 12:10). It was experienced by all of the original apostles (Acts 2:4), by new converts (Acts 10:46; 19:6), by St. Paul (I Cor. 14:18). It may be safely said that speaking in tongues was a common experience in the Apostolic Church.

2. *Speaking in tongues is prayer.* Speaking in tongues is a 'speaking unto God' (I Cor. 14:2), and therefore is essentially *prayer*. St. Paul says that he used it a great deal (I Cor. 14:18). One who speaks in tongues does not understand what he is saying; his mind is 'unfruitful' (I Cor. 14:14). But it is nevertheless edifying to pray in tongues (I Cor. 14:4), for 'the spirit prays' (I Cor. 14:14), and one 'utters mysteries in the Spirit' (I Cor. 14:2). Praying in tongues edifies (builds up) other aspects of the person than the understanding. Our experience has been that this way of praying has a profound effect on the deep feelings and attitudes which the mind cannot always directly control. And it seems to develop in one a greater sensitivity to spiritual realities than he had before.

3. *Speaking in tongues is primarily for private worship.* St. Paul suggests that he would like everyone to speak in tongues (I Cor. 14:5a)—that he himself spoke in tongues more than all (I Cor. 14:18)—but that it has limited value in a public meeting: The person who prays in a tongue would be edified, but the others would get nothing (I Cor. 14:4). Unless there is someone to interpret the tongue, the speaker is admonished to pray silently in tongues (I Cor. 14:28). The implication of these two counter-emphases is that praying in tongues is primarily personal prayer, i.e., for one's *private devotions.*

However, if an interpreter is present in a public meeting, speaking in tongues is not to be forbidden (I Cor. 14:39). Two or three utterances in tongues may be allowed in a given meeting (I Cor. 14:27). They are to be spoken in turn, i.e., one at a time, with interpretation following (I Cor. 14:27). Group praying in tongues during a public meeting—all together, out loud—is discouraged (I Cor. 14:23).

The clear purpose of I Corinthians 14 in regard to speaking in tongues is thus twofold:

a. To establish the value and blessing of praying in tongues, especially for private worship.
b. To de-emphasize and strictly discipline its use in a public meeting.

4. *Speaking in tongues is NOT a requirement for salvation.* Nowhere in Scripture is it suggested that any manifestation of the Holy Spirit is required for salvation (unless the "new birth" be thought of as a manifestation of the Holy Spirit). The formula for salvation is simply, "Believe in the Lord Jesus Christ, and you will be saved." (See Acts 16:31.) This point should be made unmistakably clear to our people. Speaking in tongues is a manifestation of the Holy Spirit which Christ set in His Church to serve a specific purpose, but one's salvation does not depend upon it.

5. *Speaking in tongues is not limited to the Apostolic Church.* No Scripture suggests that *any* of the manifestations of the Holy Spirit were meant only for the Apostolic Church. This is a purely human doctrine and rationalization to explain away the embarrassing lack of the supernatural in the Church, while still clinging to the doctrine of an inspired Scripture. Martin Luther, commenting on Mark 16:17, 18, says, "These signs [including speaking in new tongues] should be interpreted as applying to *every individual Christian*. When a person is a Christian, he has faith, and he shall also have the power to do these signs."

II. PRACTICAL ASPECTS

A. The Need for Understanding

1. *Historical abuses.* It is clear from I Corinthians 12–14 that the gift of speaking in tongues had been

abused in the Corinthian congregation. There was apparently far more of it than was necessary, and therefore St. Paul set down strict rules and limits for its use in the public meeting. During the past fifty years, speaking in tongues has been associated chiefly with the so-called Pentecostal Movement. Here, too, there have been abuses, which many Pentecostal leaders will readily admit. The former General Secretary of the Pentecostal World Conference, David du Plessis, has written, "There is not much in church services more distressing than the shocking ignorance about, and the lamentable absence of, the gifts of the Holy Spirit. Even in our Pentecostal Churches, where there is evidence of more liberty in the Spirit, we find far more physical and emotional 'reactions' to the presence of the Spirit, than true manifestations of the gifts of the Spirit. . . . I consider it heresy to speak of shaking, trembling, falling, dancing, clapping, shouting and such like actions as 'manifestations' of the Holy Spirit. These are purely human reactions to the power of the Holy Spirit and frequently hinder more than help, to bring forth genuine manifestations."

Many Christian people associate speaking in tongues with the kind of things Rev. du Plessis enumerates: shaking, trembling, shouting. Some of these associations stem from hearsay, others from actual observation. These kinds of impressions are not easily erased. St. Paul warned the Corinthians that outsiders entering their meetings would conclude that they were mad (I Cor. 14:23)—and something approaching this conclusion is what some people hold toward anything bearing the label 'Pentecostal.'

When a Christian from a historic denomination sees speaking in tongues in this light, you can understand his concern on hearing that people in his own church are speaking in tongues. He asks himself, "Is

our church going to turn into a Pentecostal camp meeting—with shouting, screaming, and carrying on?" He
sees the historical abuses connected with speaking in
tongues, and he asks whether these abuses are going
to come in and upset or pervert his traditional manner
of worship.

Those who speak in tongues need to recognize that
these objections and fears are deep-seated and real.
The danger of abuse *is* present, and one must be on
guard against it. Further, people need time to adjust
themselves to this new experience in the midst of
the congregation. If you speak in tongues, and fellow
members in the congregation fail to see in you the
marks of patience, love, and humility, they will have
every reason to doubt both the validity and the value
of your experience.

2. *Abuses not necessary or inevitable.* Philip
Hughes, writing in *Christianity Today* about the current upsurge of speaking in tongues in the denomina-
tional churches, says, "An observer of the noisiness and
unruliness which the Apostle Paul found it necessary to
rebuke in the Corinthian Church would have been disposed, understandably, to dismiss these gatherings as
something less than Christian. But he would have been
mistaken had he concluded that there was no such
thing as the spiritual gifts to which the Corinthians
laid claim. Does not Paul thank God because the Corinthian believers have been enriched in Jesus Christ in
all utterance and in all knowledge, and because they
came behind in no gift (I Cor. 1:4ff)? It is precisely
their misuse of these gifts that causes him to admon-
ish them that all things are to be done decently and
in order (14:40)."

It is clear that St. Paul did not consider the abuses
in Corinth either necessary or inevitable: He gave them

specific instructions for *curing* the abuses. Christians in other New Testament churches also spoke in tongues (see Acts 19:6), and it raised no problems as far as we know. Some people believe that since speaking in tongues is mentioned only in Corinthians, therefore it was an isolated phenomenon in that one congregation. This view, however, shows little appreciation for the actual situation in the Apostolic Church. The congregations in Corinth, Philippi, Troas, Ephesus, Colossae, and so on, were close together and had frequent fellowship with one another through the visits of various teachers and apostles (note the many personal greetings in the Epistles).

It is unlikely that this one manifestation of the Spirit would have been kept some kind of a secret in Corinth; especially when one considers how intimately this particular manifestation was tied to the original outpouring of the Holy Spirit on the Day of Pentecost. Nor is it reasonable to suppose that St. Paul, who "spoke in tongues more than all," and counted it a great blessing, would have kept this an utter secret from all believers except those in Corinth. (By following the above line of reasoning, we could as readily conclude that Holy Communion was celebrated only in Corinth, for it is not mentioned elsewhere!)

The problem in Corinth did not stem from the mere fact that they spoke in tongues, but from the fact that they lacked wisdom and guidance in the use of this gift. To say that speaking in tongues is evil or dangerous is to question the wisdom of God in placing this gift within the Church. In Corinth we witness not only an abuse of speaking in tongues, but also of Holy Communion (I Cor. 11:20–30). We do not therefore refrain from serving the Lord's Supper in our churches. A disciplined ministry of the Word will hold potential abuses in check. Our common life as

Christians would be poor indeed if we had to shun every gift of God which human beings are capable of abusing. For fear of heresy, we could not even preach the Word! The cure for abuse is not *dis*use, but *proper* use.

Those who do not speak in tongues need to recognize the distinction between the gift itself and the human abuse of the gift. The abuses you may have heard about or seen are not a necessary part of speaking in tongues. If fellow members in your congregation come into this experience, follow the counsel of I Corinthians 13:7: "Love believes all things." Believe that they will follow the *best* examples of those who speak in tongues (St. Peter, St. Paul . . .), and not the worst. Allow them time to grow into this experience, to learn its purpose and value. If they witness to a blessing in this way of worshipping God—and they abide by the guidelines laid down in the Bible—pray that God will continue to bless and guide them.

3. *Guidelines in the present movement.* The following advice of Clarence Finsaas, a Lutheran pastor, is especially appropriate for people who find themselves in one of the historic denominations:

"Revivals among Christian people usually center around the recovery of lost truths. In the Old Testament it was the recovery of the lost book, the Bible, which brought about a revival under King Josiah. In Martin Luther's time it was the recovery of that great basic truth, justification by faith. In John Wesley's day it was the truth of sanctification. In 1900 it was the discovery of the spiritual gifts that God gave to His Church which were lying dormant. This movement was called the Pentecostal movement. In seventy years it grew to nearly twelve million people. One authority calls this the 'third force in Christendom.'

"This quickening is also taking place in the framework of the historic churches. There are two streams in the moving of God's Spirit—one in the Pentecostal church and the other in the historic church. This has resulted in a better understanding between them and a fellowship such as they had not known possible.

"Many are surprised that the Holy Spirit can move also in the various traditions of the historic church. Be the church liturgical or non-liturgical, people have learned that the Holy Spirit moves in both. Whether the church doctrine has a background of Calvinism or Arminianism, this matters little, proving God is bigger than our creeds and that no denomination has a monopoly on Him.

"Problems and difficulties arise when you try to import another tradition into the church. Those Christians, especially pastors, who try to move in both streams frequently find themselves isolated in the Pentecostal setting.

"If Christians desire to serve within the framework of the historic church, they must 'earn the right to be heard.' Call it bias or prejudice, it is an unfortunate fact to be reckoned with. There are men today who long to be of service in the historic church but because they have been identified with Pentecostal groups they cannot gain a hearing in the traditional churches. This does not make the Pentecostal movement wrong or the historic churches right. Much caution and discretion is needed if we wish to share our new and fuller experience of Christ with our fellowmen. Here are some guidelines that must be observed.

"In the flush of your new spiritual experience you are carried off your feet and your judgment may be temporarily unreliable. You feel that everything is so wonderful and therefore everything that you do must be right. Certainly what you do at such times may not be the wrong action, but it may not be the wisest thing.

"If you have received a new concept of Christ which was not yours before, or if you have entered into a new fullness of the Holy Spirit, then you must share it or run the risk of losing the conscious reality of the experience. The question is how.

"You can move slowly, sharing your experience with those near you who will listen, and trust God to open up the way for more to hear you. This is the less popular route and not the very glamorous. It is the 'long haul,' but the results will be more gratifying and permanent. You will gain the ear of some who would never listen to this message, but because they trust you, they will watch you and hear you out. There will be fewer mistakes and heartaches.

"On the other hand, you can go for extravagant publicity and big meetings and be exploited and used by those who can provide the larger gatherings and you will have a good time for the present. But the inevitable time comes when your 'showcase' days are over, and then where will you go? You will discover that your friends in the historic churches may no longer want to listen to you because they feel that you have abandoned your own and their tradition.

"Thus you will sacrifice the future on the altar of the immediate and have only a very limited ministry to look forward to within your own historic tradition; but it need not be so. Consider these simple guidelines.

"1. Appreciate your historic church setting.

"2. Be aware of the great potential in terms of hungry souls within the framework of the historic church.

"3. Avoid the temptation to take the easy way where people already know your message, are sympathetic, and where the larger audiences are ready-made.

"4. Recall your own earlier prejudices and exercise patience toward your friends when you share your new-found experiences.

"5. Don't despise the 'day of small things' nor throw away your vision of what God can do.

"6. Look to God for the victory you need over bitterness because of the circumstances God has led you through to bring you to this place.

"7. Remember that no one has a corner on knowledge and that we are all erring humans and therefore must walk humbly before God and men.

"We must emphasize that the great need is to be flexible under the guidance of the Holy Spirit. Therefore these guidelines cannot be arbitrary, but general in nature. It could well be that you may get guidance that is contrary to that which has been said. Then by all means you must follow what you believe is the leading of God as long as you can square it with the Word of God.

"Christ must be the center of your life. The Bible must be your book. The gifts of the Holy Spirit are important too, but they are rather peripheral and supplemental in nature. They must never become an end in themselves. They are part of the equipment to enable us to fulfill the great commission.

"Many believe that we are on the threshold of a great awakening. God may work in these last days in a way such as He has not worked in the past. The message will be essentially the same, for His eternal Gospel cannot be changed, but the ministry will have the earmarks of the supernatural. Though this supernatural ministry is seen throughout the Bible, yet it is seen usually only through a few people at a time. The time will come when God will have a mighty army of believing people for His final thrust in world evangelism. Certainly God's children can only say to that,

'Lord, hasten the day,' and unite in prayer for this victory."

B. The Need for Pastoral Guidance

1. *For those who have NOT spoken in tongues.* The pastor must make clear to the congregation that the issue of one's salvation does *not* hinge upon speaking in tongues. If anyone begins to suggest or imply that it does, the pastor must speak to such a person and handle it as he would any other false teaching in the congregation—with love and understanding, but also with firmness. No one's assurance of salvation should ever be put in jeopardy by the erroneous teaching that you must speak in tongues in order to be saved.

On the other hand, the pastor must also make clear to the congregation that speaking in tongues is clearly spoken about in Scripture, and that those who speak in tongues have biblical sanction for doing so. The implication must never be allowed to stand that speaking in tongues—properly ordered—is a departure from sound doctrine. Members of the congregation who have not experienced speaking in tongues should be pointedly discouraged from disparaging the gift, as such, or any fellow member who has received it. Nor should it be allowed that the proper use of the gift be discouraged in the church. If the Lord has seen fit to bestow this gift on members of the congregation, that is all the evidence Scripture requires, that it shall have its place in the life of the congregation—the place allowed it by Scripture. To despise, or even to take lightly, a gift of the Holy Spirit is to put oneself in grave spiritual danger. And speaking in tongues is clearly designated in Scripture as a gift of the Holy Spirit. If some people in the congregation find this disturbing, the pastor can point out to them that except for its occasional use in a group meeting, speaking in tongues is primarily for private worship, and is therefore a matter between the individual and God. No member of the congregation should call into question or criticism the personal devotional life of another member.

Renewal Magazine, published in England, recorded the story of an Anglican parish in New Zealand, whose priest offered the following wise counsel to his parishioners:

"There is a spiritual phenomenon taking place in our parish which is giving some folk considerable concern. You may hear it referred to as 'the Baptism in the Holy Spirit.'

"You may be one of those whose only knowledge of this is some vague, queer story of peculiar goings-on. There are those who have never heard of it; there are those who are interested and those who are downright antagonistic.

"Before I say what I want to, I would ask you to bear in mind that many of our experiences are hard to explain, especially on the spiritual level. . . . As soon as someone in our midst has an encounter with the Lord Jesus Christ and is prepared to sit up all hours making a study of this new-found love and faith by reading the Scriptures and through praying, there are those whose first reaction is to say that the person is emotionally unstable. When something a little unorthodox happens there are those, and generally good church people, who want to condemn—certainly not to pray. Why is this? I suggest to you that it is for the same reasons as the Jews rejected Jesus; they did not like His message and it was not what they expected.

"We are seriously warned in the Bible not to grieve the Holy Spirit—but I just do not know of any better way of grieving the Holy Spirit than to reject and condemn His activity in our midst. One will always

hear of the sensational and unusual happenings because
that is just human nature and we lap it up. But I am
afraid we do not always wish to hear the useful and
positive sides; sometimes we do not really wish to get
to the bottom of something and hear the truth—because
we think it is not what we expected and it is not acceptable.

"If you feel that you disagree with the whole matter
of the Baptism in the Holy Spirit (and you are perfectly entitled to do so), even so, your greatest con-
tribution to the life of this parish will be through
prayer—and not criticism. If the people who are
seeking and experiencing this gift are as stupid as some
folk think they are, then they most certainly need
your prayers. But if you are genuinely in doubt, then
ask God to show you—I really mean this—*ask* God
to show you. This is something about which we hear
very little, the subject of 'Listening to God.' We say
to God—please God do this and do that and show me
how to do something or other else—but we do not
wait long enough to give God a chance to get an answer
through to us. It is an interesting fact that God gave
us two ears and only one tongue—and maybe He
intended that we should listen twice as much as we
talk! Jesus said, 'If you then, who are evil, know how
to give good gifts to your children, how much more
will the heavenly Father give the Holy Spirit to
those who ask him' (Luke 11:13)."

2. *For those who HAVE spoken in tongues.* The
experience of speaking in tongues often effects a deep
revitalizing of one's faith. The pastor can help a person
set the experience in its proper context with some
practical suggestions such as these:

　　a. Remember, speaking in tongues does not make
　　　　you a mature and seasoned Christian overnight.

It is a *tool*, to be used faithfully in your daily prayers as one means of attaining to maturity. At first you may experience considerable joy and exuberance in the practice of the gift, because it is something new. Later, it will settle more into a quiet routine. This does not mean that you have 'lost something.' It just means that you have moved into the next phase; your 'new tongue' is becoming almost second nature to you. Its purpose is not to give you a continual thrill, but rather to provide you with one more way—a wonderful, God-given way—for Christ to become formed in you.

b. Use this gift primarily in your private devotions. St. Paul says that one who speaks in tongues *edifies himself*. Speaking in tongues opens up a new dimension in personal prayer, which can effect deep changes and blessings in your Christian life. For the most part, this is not a gift to be displayed openly, but is a private language of adoration, praise, devotion, and intercession between you and God.

c. Be modest and quiet about your own experience. Some of the other members in the congregation may find speaking in tongues hard to accept. Talk and argument will not help. This blessing cannot be forced on anyone, nor should any 'pressure' ever be applied. If an opportunity presents itself, share your testimony in a simple way—and then let the Lord use it in His own way with that individual.

d. Seek fellowship with others who share your joy and enthusiasm in this blessing. But guard against forming any 'cliques' within the congregation. Prayer meetings and group get-togethers should generally be open to any member of the con-

gregation. Beware of spiritual pride. (See I Corinthians 4:7.)

e. Make certain that the testimony of your *words*
is backed up by the testimony of your *life*. The
most convincing evidence that you have truly received a blessing from the Lord is the effect
which it comes to have on your everyday life.
Be on hand when there is *work* to do in the congregation—humble, obscure tasks that need to
be done, but which often get little recognition.
Practical work is a necessary 'balance wheel'
in the spiritual life; you can't live on a solid
diet of prayer meetings and Bible study. Furthermore, this is one of the most effective testimonies
you can make in the congregation. The sight
of a man painting a Sunday school room, or a
woman hanging new curtains in the church
kitchen is worth a hundred testimonies. Unconsciously your fellow members will say, "There
must be something to it, all right. When there's
a job to do, you can always count on them."

f. In our experience, it has been observed that
those who receive the baptism with the Holy
Spirit, and speak in tongues, also quite generally
accept the biblical standard of the tithe. Steward-
ship of money is one of the most accurate barom-
eters of spiritual life which we have. It is no
accident that Jesus spoke about the stewardship
of material possessions more than any other
subject. Make certain that a full tithe (10%) of
your income is given to the Lord's work. It is
'God's financial plan' for a Christian to live on
90% of his income; God blesses the tither (Mal.
3:10). Here, again, is a place for you to give
silent testimony to the genuineness of your encounter with the Lord.

3. *For the congregation as a whole.* The local congregation may need to set up some ground rules, and these could vary considerably from congregation to congregation. In no case, of course, should these local guidelines be at variance with the spirit and intent of Scripture. The following is simply a summary of the experience in our own congregation:

a. We do not encourage speaking in tongues during the regular Sunday worship service, although it surely is not forbidden. It seems more appropriate, however, at an informal evening meeting or a prayer group.

b. Occasionally in a prayer group someone will speak in tongues, with the interpretation following. Those who come to the prayer groups expect this, and it is done decently and in order.

c. We prefer to have these prayer groups meet either in the church, or in the home of one who is clearly recognized as a responsible leader in the congregation. It has been suggested that those who object to speaking in tongues would be mollified if the meetings were not identified with the church. But this would tend toward the very thing we want to avoid—the splitting up of the congregation into little independent cliques. If we turn speaking in tongues out of the Church, there is a very real danger of turning it over to the devil. The very thing which this gift needs—pastoral guidance and the discipline of the Church—would be diminished. Let it be done completely in the open. No one is forced to come to this kind of a group, but anyone is welcome.

d. We discourage the copying of any set of traditions, customs, or mannerisms in our prayer groups. We have nothing against these traditions from other Christian groups, but we do not feel that they are essential to the manifestation of the gifts of the Spirit in our setting. It is unnatural for our people to pray in loud voices, or to intersperse another person's prayer with frequent "Amen's" or "Hallelujah's." This does not mean that we advocate a sterile and inflexible adherence to our own worship traditions either. Over the period of several years, we have seen the Spirit lead us into many new forms of worship, and we are always happy when He does this. The point is, that *He* does it. We feel that this makes for a healthier growth in worship, than artificially to import mannerisms of worship from other traditions.

e. We encourage each person in the congregation to come to his own decision regarding speaking in tongues. The question is not, "What should the *congregation* do about speaking in tongues?" (except in regard to the ordering of it in group meetings), but the question is, "Lord, what should *I* do about speaking in tongues?"

When a person feels that this experience is not for him, that the Holy Spirit is working in his life in other ways, that is his decision, and there should be no implication that he is "less of a Christian" than someone else who speaks in tongues. In fact, it misses the whole spirit of I Corinthians 12 to compare one Christian to another in such a way. We are members of His Body—each one unique, each one dealt with by the Lord in an individual way.

On the other hand, when a person feels that this blessing is something he needs in order to become a more effective Christian, then we pray that he may receive it. When the Lord has led him to that decision, we believe that he will become a better Christian— not better than someone else, but better than he himself was before. For surely one cannot receive the grace of God, receive any special blessing or enduement from God, without it making a difference in his Christian life.

4

speaking in tongues
as 'ministry'

*The Significance of Speaking in Tongues as It Relates
to Other Gifts and Ministries in the Body of Christ*

In the foregoing chapters we used the microscope, as it were: We focused upon the gift of tongues and examined it at close range. We considered how it relates to one's initiatory experience of receiving the baptism with the Holy Spirit, and then how it functions in one's private devotional life. In this chapter we want to step back and see it in a broader perspective. For speaking in tongues is a gift which operates within the Body of Christ *in coordination with other gifts and ministries*—"for the equipment of the saints, for the work of the ministry, for building up the body of Christ" (Eph. 4:12).

A display of spiritual pyrotechnics, just to show off one's spiritual virtuosity, finds no echo of encouragement in I Corinthians 12–14. Such a display would be something like a person who has learned how to pat his head and rub his stomach at the same time. It is an interesting feat of coordination, but serves no real purpose. The picture in these chapters of the Bible is rather one of a smoothly coordinated athlete— every member of his body functioning in harmony to accomplish a given and worthwhile objective.

Think of a swimmer poised at pool's edge for the 50-yard free style. His eyes are trained down the pool toward the finish mark. His ears are keyed for the starter's gun. His thigh muscles tense for the dive. The starter gun sounds. He hits the water with a splash. His arms and legs go into action, carrying the greater share of the responsibility for the next few moments. His breathing, usually a rhythmic and regular function, humbly sets its function aside so the head can remain in the water. His whole body churns through the water. Inside, the functioning of the heart and blood match their service to the body's need of the moment. The swimmer slaps in on the finish line. Legs and arms come to rest. The breathing goes into normal operation again. The body has finished one task—and begins another. We might find ourselves remarking about the swimmer's terrific arm action, or his powerful kick. But we know that the work of the arms and legs is made possible only by the coordinated support of the entire body. This has been an effort and a victory for the whole body!

This is the kind of picture which we have of the Church in I Corinthians 12–14: a Body with many different members, all functioning in coordination to care for one another, and to accomplish the purpose and goal of the Body as a whole. This is the sense of the 12th chapter, beginning with verse 14, and ending with these words in verse 27: "Now you [plural, i.e., *all of you together*] are the body of Christ and individually members of it."

With this concept of the Body as a backdrop, we want to look at the inter-related functioning of the various gifts and ministries within the Body of Christ—including the gift of tongues. To survey this conveniently, we consider it under the aspect of three words: Motive, Manifestation, and Ministry.

Motive

The motive for the coordinated action of the Body—and the motive for the activity of each individual member—is given in the 13th chapter: *love.*

It is surely no accident that this great chapter of Scripture is set down right in the middle of Paul's discussion of the spiritual gifts—between the theory of the 12th chapter and the practical applications of the 14th chapter. Because it is love—the divine *agape,* "poured into our hearts through the Holy Spirit which has been given to us" (Rom. 5:5)—which controls the use of every spiritual gift, integrating it into the total life and ministry of the Body. The Apostle Paul uses strong language in the first three verses of the 13th chapter toward those who would use gifts of the Spirit for the purpose of self-exaltation. According to God's valuation, a gifted member—no matter how spectacular or even effective he may be in exercising his gift—is *nothing,* unless he uses the gift in love. *A gift is always to be used with an eye to the Body—*to the upbuilding of the Body itself, or to the Body's ministry outward.

You frequently hear it said that "love is the greatest of the gifts." The implication seems to be that we should spend our greatest effort toward acquiring and manifesting this gift, and that if we have love, the other gifts become more or less optional or incidental. In a broad sense this may be said. But in this particular context it tends to be misleading. Strictly speaking, love is not a *gift* of the Spirit, but a *fruit* of the Spirit (Gal. 5:22). The word *charisma* is never used to denote love, as it is used to denote healing, miracles, tongues, and so forth. If we lump love together with these other gifts and ministries which Paul is speaking about, we miss the distinctive position which love holds in the entire discussion: We make it an *alternative* to the other spiritual gifts, whereas the Apostle clearly sets it above all of the gifts—not as an alternative, but as a *controlling principle*.

Structurally, the 13th chapter is set between the 12 and the 14th chapters as a kind of extended parentheses. You can move from the end of chapter 12 directly to the beginning of chapter 14 with no break in logic, thought, or grammar. The Apostle's line of thought comes out with great clarity when you do this, reading 12:27–31 ( ) 14:1:

> Now you are the body of Christ and individually members of it. And God has appointed in the church first apostles, second prophets, third teachers, then workers of miracles, then healers, helpers, administrators, speakers in various kinds of tongues. Are all apostles? Are all prophets? Are all teachers? Do all work miracles? Do all possess gifts of healing? Do all speak with tongues? Do all interpret? But earnestly desire the higher gifts.
>
> And I will show you a still more excellent way: Make love your aim, and earnestly desire the spiritual gifts, especially that you may prophesy.

This reading helps clarify a point which is often clouded with misunderstanding. The "more excellent way" which Paul advocates is not love as an alternative to the use of spiritual gifts. It is rather, *love as a more adequate motive for obtaining and using the gifts*—more adequate than mere desire: ". . . earnestly desire the higher gifts. And I will show you a still more excellent way [than merely desiring them]: Make love your aim AND earnestly desire the spiritual gifts. . . ." It is not love *instead of* the desire for spiritual

gifts, but love *together with* the desire for spiritual
gifts which the Apostle advocates.

This only makes good common sense when we
stop to think about it. If the love of Christ dwells in
your heart, you are going to desire earnestly anything
which will help you express that love in a concrete
and effective way.

Suppose a man is dying of thirst in the desert, and
you are sent out to rescue him. Out you go, your heart
overflowing with love and concern. You find the man.
His tongue and lips are swollen. "Water! Water!" he
gasps frantically. But you just go up and throw your
arms around him and say, "Oh, we don't believe in
the gifts, brother. We just want to *love you.*"

The gifts are not a (lower) alternative to love.
They are the very means which the Spirit has given
us to express Christ's love in an effective and concrete
way. Desiring the spiritual gifts is not a sign of spiritual
immaturity, acceptable only in someone who has not
yet learned the more excellent way of love. Rather,
desire for the spiritual gifts is a sign that one *does*
love—but knows that in himself he has nothing to give.
He is like the 'friend at midnight' (Luke 11:5ff.). He
goes to God and says, "This friend of mine has come,
and I have nothing to give him. I pray you, supply
me with what he needs, that I may give it to him."
He doesn't sit in his rocker, piously saying, "If the
Lord wants to give me any gifts, He will do it." No,
he *goes*. He *asks*—until he receives. He *seeks*—until
he finds. He *knocks*—until the door is opened. This
is the wedding of love and desire which the Apostle
urges upon us in these chapters of First Corinthians.

In I Corinthians 12:8–11, St. Paul lists nine gifts
or manifestations of the Holy Spirit. The essential
aspect of each of these gifts is well defined in the
German publication *Gnadengaben*, a commentary on

I Corinthians 12–14 by Arnold Bittlinger:

1. *The Word of Wisdom.* In a difficult or dangerous situation, a Christian will be given a word of wisdom which solves the problem, or silences an opponent. This is not the same as the wisdom which an individual has acquired through experience. It is, rather, a "word" of wisdom, which will be given to various members of the congregation according to need.
2. *The Word of Knowledge.* This gift reveals facts from the natural or supernatural world, which a Christian would not be able to know by normal means.
3. *Faith.* This is not the "faith unto salvation" which every Christian has, nor the "fruit of the Spirit" (Gal. 5:22), which every Christian should bring forth, but this is 'mountain-moving faith' (Matt. 17:20; I Cor. 13:2), which individual Christians may manifest as a gift of the Spirit.
4. *Healing.* The main thrust of this gift is toward the healing of the body from physical infirmity. Beyond that, however, it would apply to the healing of 'the whole man'—body, soul and spirit.
5. *Miracles.* This gift goes beyond the miraculous healing of the body to include miracles of every sort. The object of the miracle is determined by the situation and need of the moment.
6. *Prophecy.* The primary emphasis in this gift is not upon prediction of future events, but upon an appropriate and needed word in the present situation— a word of upbuilding, encouragement, consolation (I Cor. 14:3). This word, of course, may well include a glance either into the past or into the future.
7. *Discernment of Spirits.* This gift enables the Church of Christ and her members to distinguish between

divine, human, and demonic powers—to discern the
source of a particular utterance or action.

8. *Speaking in Tongues.* Through this gift, the exalted
Lord gives the members of His Church the power
to 'express the inexpressible,' and praise God in new
speech.

9. *Interpretation.* This is a 'sister gift' which makes
it possible and useful for the gift of tongues to be
used in a group meeting. Interpretation is not an
exact 'translation' of the utterance in tongues, nor
a commentary upon it, but is a rendering in the
vernacular of the content or 'gist' of the utterance
in tongues. The one who speaks in tongues speaks
to God; the one who interprets receives the interpretation from God.

Consider with what absolute legitimacy one might
earnestly desire and seek any one of these gifts, *motivated by love.* If there is someone in the congregation
who is confused and uncertain about the truth of the
Gospel, or who has a personal problem, what more loving thing could you do than deliver to such a one the
Spirit's word of wisdom for that particular need? If
the congregation is in a state of spiritual lethargy or
disillusionment, what more loving thing could you do
than deliver to them a prophetic word—an exhortation
from the Spirit? If a member is sick, what more loving
thing could you do than deliver to him the healing
power of Christ? If the congregation is under pointed
attack by the principalities and powers, the spiritual
hosts of wickedness, what more loving thing could you
do than to discern their presence, and with the authority of the Name of Jesus stand against them? Yes, even
the gift of tongues: If you are called to edify the congregation, what more loving thing could you do than
first go into your private prayer closet and let the

Lord edify you—speak ten thousand words in a tongue, if need be—so that when you come to church you will be so edified that five words with the mind will be spiritual dynamite. This is the logical way to interpret St. Paul's words in I Corinthians 14:18-19: "I thank God that I speak in tongues more than you all; nevertheless, *in church* I would rather speak five words with my mind, in order to instruct others, than ten thousand in a tongue."

Because he loved, St. Paul spoke in tongues more than them all. He knew that in this gift God had given him a supernatural tool for edification. Faithfully used, it would enable him better to guide and edify those under his charge. But because it was *love* which motivated him—and not the desire to show off spiritually—this gift was one which he used primarily, perhaps exclusively, in his private worship. Whatever the Lord wrought in private would inevitably bless the churches as Paul continued to move among them in his appointed calling.

It is not too much to say that there is a direct ratio between love and desire: The greater place which the love of Christ has in our hearts, the greater will be our desire for the gifts of the Spirit, through which we may effectively express that love.

Manifestation

When the Body of Christ is functioning in a normal way—normal by New Testament standards—the gifts of the Spirit which Paul lists in I Corinthians 12 will come into manifestation . . . as they are needed. Our key to understanding and visualizing the way in which this works is in verse 7: "To each is given the manifestation of the Spirit for the common good." The picture given us is this: The Holy Spirit has a supply of

gifts. He gives these to various members of the congregation. But the gift is not for the private benefit of
the one who receives it: The member is a 'manifester'
of the gift. He holds it in trust, and at the proper time
administers it, for the benefit of the Body. He receives
it in order to manifest it—deliver it—to the one for
whom it is ultimately intended. Only when it comes
to that person does it become, in the true sense, a "gift."

Consider, for example, a person who is sick. The
Spirit gives, or has given, "gifts of healing" to a member
of the congregation. This person goes to the sick member and manifests the gift which the Spirit has entrusted
to him—and the sick person receives healing.

The word of wisdom and the word of knowledge
operate in a similar way. The gift, as we have seen, is
not designated 'wisdom' or 'knowledge' *per se*, but a
word (or "utterance") of wisdom or knowledge. The
person who manifests one of these gifts has received a
word or an utterance. By the Spirit, he has been granted
momentary access to a tiny segment of God's infinite
wisdom or knowledge. To the one who manifests it, it
may seem a rather ordinary "word"—a thought, idea,
or illustration which is impressed upon his mind. But
for the one who receives it—the one for whom it is
intended—it is truly a word of wisdom or a word of
knowledge.

A Baptist minister had fellowship with one of our
prayer groups off and on over a period of about a year.
He had begun to hold healing services in his church,
and the Lord honored that ministry almost at once with
some definite healings. Some of his fellow pastors looked
a bit askance at this whole business, and he questioned
whether he should continue. He came to the prayer
group one day with this question very much on his
mind, though he didn't speak of it openly. During the
meeting, one of the members of the prayer group re-

ceived an utterance in the Spirit and spoke it out in a simple and unspectacular way. The sense of it was this: "I am with you on the road you are travelling. Do not be afraid of what others may think. I will sustain and guide you." To the member who spoke the words, it was merely an utterance. To the Baptist minister, for whom it was intended, it was a word of encouragement, a definite and pointed answer to the prayer of his heart. He later told of the encouragement which this word had given him, and how it had been confirmed in events which followed; the ministry of healing not only continued to bless the congregation, but a more open and positive attitude also developed among his fellow pastors.

A rather interesting and unusual example of the word of knowledge is told by David du Plessis. He was scheduled to give a lecture at a theological seminary. A theologian on the faculty let it be known that he was going to 'make this Pentecostal tumble.' He planned to needle him with some thorny questions. Some of the students wrote and warned du Plessis about it beforehand. He came and gave his lecture. Afterward the theologian asked a question. At the time, du Plessis did not know that it was the man who had promised to make trouble for him, for they hadn't been introduced beforehand. The question was a good one and he answered it. He went on to say, "Now that question actually involves another question—" He stated the second question rhetorically, and answered it. That suggested to him yet a third and a fourth question, which he stated and answered in the same fashion. The theologian then asked another question along another line altogether. Du Plessis answered it. He then suggested that this, too, involved a second . . . and a third . . . and a fourth question. So he proceeded to answer again in the same way. After that no more questions were raised, and the meeting was dismissed. The next morning some of the students came to him and said, "A miracle has happened! The students were up until two and three o'clock in the morning, reading the Bible and praying together."

Du Plessis said that he thought that was wonderful. Then he asked, "But what happened to your theologian who was going to give me such a bad time?"

"Didn't you know?" they asked. "He was the one who asked you the question after the lecture."

"Those were decent enough questions," du Plessis said.

"That's what we thought, too," the students said, "so we went and asked him why he hadn't tried to needle you like he said he was going to. He said, 'What can you do with a man like that? I asked him my first question and he proceeded to answer the next three questions I had written down on my paper. I thought that he was probably brilliant in that line, so I tried something else. He proceeded to answer the next three questions I had written down on my paper. I gave up!' "

As far as du Plessis was concerned, he was giving a normal answer to a question, as it came to him. But the Spirit knew what the theologian had written down. Finding in du Plessis an instrument, He used a 'word of knowledge' as a special sign to silence a contentious spirit. Du Plessis might never have known that he had manifested a word of knowledge in this specific instance, if the students had not told him about it. He puts its succinctly thus: "As you begin more and more to live in this realm of spiritual awareness, you become 'naturally supernatural.' "

This experience may seem a little extraordinary, and yet every pastor has known something akin to it in his own experience. A parishioner comes up after a service and says, "You must have been reading my

mind today, Pastor. You were speaking right to me!"
And then the person may cite a particular phrase or
illustration which came in quite 'by the way.' We need
to expect this to happen when we stand up to preach
God's Word. As St. Paul said, "My message was not
in plausible words of wisdom, but in demonstration of
the Spirit and power, that your faith might not rest
in the wisdom of men but in the power of God" (I Cor.
2:4–5).

Whenever gifts of the Spirit come into evidence,
Satan will be close at hand trying his worst to pervert
or counterfeit the operation of the Spirit. The first line
of defense against the devil is the Scripture. A congregation well grounded in Scripture will put the devil
to some tests which he won't be able to pass. But even
beyond this, the Spirit has provided a special gift to
protect the flock from wolves who would come in to
upset the work of the Spirit: the gift of the discernment
of spirits. This is necessary because of the extreme sub-
tlety of the spirits. The slave girl in Acts 16 followed
after Paul and Silas crying, "These men are servants
of the Most High God who proclaim to you the way
of salvation." What she said was absolutely true, and
yet she was speaking by a wrong spirit. Paul discerned
this, and cast the spirit out.

A neighboring pastor told us about an experience
which he once had with the discernment of spirits. Two
strange women came to his church one day, and in the
course of the meeting stood up and prophesied. The
words were scriptural, and yet he felt like a whole
battery of fire alarms started to go off inside him. He
leaned over to an older pastor who was sitting next to
him, and said, "What is it about those women?" The
older pastor answered, "The words they are saying are
true, but the spirit is false." The pastor of the church
said that before the next meeting he prayed to God

and said, "If You want to shut them up, you can;
but if You don't, I will." He stood at the door to inter-
cept them, with the intention of telling them that they
were welcome to worship, but that they could not
minister in the service. Interestingly enough, they
never came back.

In a public meeting, the gift of tongues is designed
to operate with the sister-gift of interpretation. The
pattern is exactly the same as with the other gifts
which we have mentioned. A person receives an
utterance, and manifests it *for the good of the Body*.
The tongue plus the interpretation will be edifying for the church, just as a well-chosen prayer
in English edifies the whole congregation. And it has
added power: It lends a distinct note of the supernatural to the meeting. We have seen prayer meetings suddenly lifted from the doldrums to the heavenlies
by one brief utterance in tongues with the interpretation following. Tongues actually has limited use
in group meetings, but that use should not be diminished
or ignored. God has made specific and undeniable pro-
vision for the public use of tongues by providing the
sister-gift of interpretation. He has further protected
this with the specific word, "Do not forbid speaking in
tongues" (I Cor. 14:39).

The gifts of tongues and interpretation illustrate
the basic inter-relatedness of the manifestations of the
Spirit. When the Body has a specific need or task, two
or even three gifts might come into operation to take
care of it. In the case of sickness, for instance, a word
of knowledge might be manifested to point out the *cause*
of the sickness before healing can be effected. Or suppose that a disturbed member is under attack by satanic
forces: This would have to be discerned and dealt with
before a word of wisdom could even get through to such
a person.

The Holy Spirit broods over the flock of God with watchful eye, determining with absolute wisdom the need of each member, as well as the needs of the group, and then gives gifts to meet those needs—*to the extent that He finds members yielded to His moving, ready to manifest the gifts which He apportions as He wills.*

Ministry

The word 'minister' has become a singular rather than a plural concept in our thinking. In everyday usage it means just one person—the pastor of a congregation. In the New Testament, a pastor was simply one minister among many. His specific ministry was one of overseeing and teaching. But alongside of this pastoral ministry were ministries of prophecy, ministries of healing, ministries of serving, ministries of exhortation—each ministry carried on by an individual or individuals whom God had appointed to that specific ministry in the Body of Christ.

What a day it would be if, when the fall Sunday school program begins, the Board of Education would not have to look at one another with pained expressions and say, "Who can we get to teach Sunday school this year?"—but would simply recognize and call out of the congregation those whom God had anointed and appointed to the ministry of teaching. How many backslidden church members might be reclaimed if a Spirit-anointed ministry of exhortation were operative among us? The ministry in a normal New Testament congregation was a Body ministry, each member contributing his unique ministry toward the upbuilding and work of the Body.

In Corinth Paul had to deal with a group of Christians whose aim was spiritual virtuosity, rather than humble service in the Body of Christ. He leveled at them his famous barrage of rhetorical questions: "Are all apostles? Are all prophets? Are all teachers? Do all work miracles? Do all possess gifts of healing? Do all speak with tongues? Do all interpret?" But what would St. Paul say if he were to walk into one of our churches today? Might he not look around, raise a quizzical eyebrow, and ask, "Do *any* possess gifts of healing? Do *any* work miracles? Do *any* speak with tongues? Do *any* interpret?"

Whether you, as an individual, possess gifts of healing, whether you as an individual work miracles, whether you as an individual bring utterances in tongues is not of primary importance. But it is of critical importance that each of these appointed ministries be desired, sought after, prayed for, and received *in the congregation.* The Body of Christ, in its local expression, is weakened and crippled to the extent that any one of these ministries becomes atrophied. Conversely, the Body functions in power and with truly spiritual results to the extent that all of these ministries are brought into coordinated action.

5

is speaking in tongues
for me?

How a Believer May Receive This Blessing

Weymouth's translation of Acts 2:4 pinpoints what actually happens when a person speaks in tongues: "They were all filled with the Holy Spirit, and began to speak in other tongues according *as the Spirit gave them words to utter.*" Many people expect to be seized upon, overwhelmed, and virtually compelled to speak in tongues. But this is not the way the Spirit treats us. He leads, He encourages, He prompts, He gives— but He does not force.

The prompting may be a syllable, a word, or a phrase in the mind; to the understanding it is a meaningless sound, but when spoken out it leads into a new tongue. Or, it may be a certain 'moving of the Spirit' upon the tongue or lips, which will form into syllables and words as one lends the voice. Or, it may be a spontaneous speaking forth difficult to describe, because it is so personal. People's experience of just how it begins seems to vary greatly. Once begun, however, the phenomenon is fairly consistent: A spontaneous and usually fluent language, in which the words are prompted not by the mind but by the Spirit.

Is this experience for *any* Christian? To be even more specific, is it for *me?* Can *I* speak in tongues?

It is significant that in the Book of Acts they *all*

received the Holy Spirit—and spoke in tongues. In
I Corinthians 12:30, St. Paul suggests that all do not
speak in tongues, but this refers to the use of the gift
in the church. (See verse 28.) This, of course, is true,
as we pointed out in the previous chapter. In a church
meeting only certain ones will be led to bring an
utterance in tongues. But, while God will appoint
only certain ones to speak in tongues in a gathered
assembly, *every* believer can be blessed by the self-
edification which this gift brings in private devotions.
We believe that any Christian who earnestly desires
this blessing may ask the Lord for it, and receive it.
(See Luke 11:5–13; Matt. 7:7–11.)

It is not likely, however, that you will receive this
blessing unless you do *desire* it. Some people say, "If
God wants me to have the gift of speaking in tongues,
then He will give it to me." This reflects a certain
piety on the surface, but this is not the way God
deals with us. God does not force His gifts upon us.
He makes them available, then encourages us to "ask. . .
seek . . . knock." In I Corinthians 14:1, we are specifically commanded to "earnestly desire spiritual gifts,"
for unless there is the hunger of desire, there is no real
receptivity. Those who have a deep hunger for God, and
are prepared to seek earnestly the fulfillment of that
hunger without any qualifications except those im-
posed by Scripture itself, receive this blessing the
most readily.

Speaking in tongues is essentially *an act of faith.*
An act of faith involves two things: The act of the
believer, and the response of God. An act of faith
always involves a venture, a 'risk.' Arnold Bittlinger
makes the following appropriate observation:

"In Joshua 3:8, 9, 13 we read how the Lord tells
Joshua, 'You shall command the priests who bear the
ark of the covenant, "When you come to the brink

of the waters of the Jordan, you shall stand still in
the Jordan." And Joshua said to the people of Israel,
"When the soles of the feet of the priests who bear
the ark of the Lord, the Lord of all the earth, shall rest
in the waters of the Jordan, the waters of the Jordan
shall be stopped from flowing, and the waters coming
down from above shall stand in one heap." '

"The priests actually had to dip their feet in the
brink of the water," Bittlinger points out. "That was
their act of faith. It involved a risk: The risk of getting
all wet and looking foolish before the people, should
God fail to keep His side of the bargain! But when they
took this step of faith, God stopped up the waters (Joshua 3:16).

"Speaking in tongues is a venture of faith. You
lay aside any language which you have ever learned,
then lift up your voice and speak out. The 'risk' is
that you will say nothing more than bla-bla-bla. But
when you take this step of simple faith, you discover that
God indeed keeps His side of the bargain, and begins
to shape the sound which you continue to give Him
into a language of prayer and praise."

Fear is sometimes expressed that people may be
'coached' into an experience of speaking in tongues.
There is indeed a need for wisdom and restraint at
this point. The fear, however, is probably exaggerated.
A person may be coached into starting to speak in
tongues, but he can hardly be coached into a *continu-
ing experience* of the gift. Precisely how a person begins
speaking in tongues is not as important as how he continues to use the gift day by day.

The fear that one may be coached into an experience of speaking in tongues may also stem from a
false starting-point. One supposes that this involves
an attempt to 'put something over'—either on God, or
on the person who seeks the gift. The implication is

that God is not really ready to give the gift, and that
man is trying to sneak it away. The problem, however,
is actually the reverse. God is more than ready to
bestow the gift, but we are often so bound and inept
that we do not know how to receive it.

We encounter this same sort of thing in other areas
of the Christian Faith. On occasion, for instance, we
find it helpful to 'coach' a person in regard to conversion. The person genuinely wants to accept Christ,
but cannot seem to put it into words. So we pray a
simple prayer of repentance and faith, inviting him
to repeat it after us. He does, and we accept this as
a genuine beginning. The proof of it, of course, must
be that he goes on from that point to believe and
live as a real Christian.

Of course the kind of help which one gives to
a person in regard to conversion is not the same
as for a person seeking the gift of tongues. (One would
not receive the gift of tongues merely by repeating
someone *else's* utterances in tongues.) An encouragement to the person to 'speak out in faith, and God
will shape the sound which you give Him into a
language of prayer and praise'—this might be deemed
a 'coaching' of the person. The advice of Arnold Bittlinger cited above, could be looked upon in the same
light. But is this actually any more so than telling
a person step-by-step how to 'invite Christ into your
heart'? The more searching question must be asked:
What happens *afterward* in the lives of the people
who pray for and receive the gift of tongues with
some such help or encouragement as this? If the gift
becomes knit into their prayer life in a wholesome
way, and brings forth the fruit of edification, then we
cannot score too seriously the particular way in which
they prayed for and received the gift.

Most people, however, can come into this blessing

in a simple and natural way, without too much attention to 'mechanics.' A few simple steps are often a helpful preparation:

1. Search the Scriptures. Be convinced in your own mind and heart that this gift is from God, is intended for the Church today, and is available to you. Consider these clear truths of Scripture:

    a. God tells us to earnestly desire the spiritual gifts (I Cor. 14:1).

    b. God delights to give good gifts to His children (Matt. 7:11).

    c. The baptism with the Holy Spirit, with the manifestation of speaking in tongues, was for *all* believers (Acts 2:4; 10:44–46; 19:6).

    d. This is a gift which *every believer* can use with benefit. If a member of the church is sick, it is not necessary that every member have the gift of healing; one member with the gift would be sufficient. *Every* member, however, needs to maintain a *private devotional life*, and therefore every member can benefit from this wonderful gift. The main blessing of the gift of tongues is in one's private devotions. The Lord, speaking by the Apostle Paul, says, "I want you *all* to speak in tongues" (I Cor. 14:5).

2. Ask yourself, "Why do I want this blessing?" It is a part of what you may receive through receiving the baptism with the Holy Spirit, and Christ tells us what that is for in Acts 1:8, "You shall be my witnesses." If you yearn to be a better witness for Christ, for Him to have a deeper grip on your life, this blessing is for you.

3. Put it to the Lord in prayer. Tell Him the desire of your heart, and ask Him to guide you. You may

feel led to wait a time, or you may feel ready at once
to seek the blessing.

Often it is a help to seek out someone who already
has experienced the blessing, and have him pray with
you (see Acts 8:15). Many people, however, have
received all by themselves in their own prayer closets.

4. In order to speak in tongues, you must quit
speaking in any other language which you know, for
you cannot speak two languages at once. After you
have come to the Lord with prayers and petitions in
your native tongue, lapse into silence and resolve
to speak not a syllable of any language you have
learned. Focus your thoughts on Christ. *Then simply
lift up your voice and speak out confidently*, in the
faith that the Lord will take the sound which you give
Him, and shape it into a language. Take no particular
thought of what you are saying, for your mind is
'unfruitful' during the exercise of this gift. As far as
you are concerned, it will be just a series of sounds.
The first syllables and words may sound strange to
your ear. They may be halting and inarticulate. You
may have the thought that you are just making it up.
But as you *continue to speak in faith*, 'boldly, confidently, and with enthusiasm' (literal rendering of Acts 2:4),
and as the lips and tongue begin to move more freely,
the Spirit will shape for you a language of prayer and
praise which will be beautiful to the ears of the Lord!

The initial hurdle to speaking in tongues, it seems,
is simply this realization that *you* must 'speak forth.'
(Many people wait and wait for something to 'happen,'
not realizing that the Holy Spirit is waiting for them
to speak out in faith!) Once this initial hurdle is
cleared, however, you will find your spirit wonderfully
released to worship the Lord as your tongue speaks
this new language of worship.

Once a person has spoken in tongues, he may do

so at will thereafter. Two 'testings' of this gift seem
almost universal, and a word concerning them may
save those who are new in the gift some needless
anxiety.

The first test usually comes almost at once: It is
the temptation to think, "I am just making this up."
This is a natural thought, for the inter-action between
the believer and the Holy Spirit is so subtle that it
is hard to draw a clear line between my speaking
and His prompting. The temptation, when this thought
comes, is to draw back and deny the gift, or to quit
using it. Our ultimate confidence cannot be the experience itself, but God's Word: He has spoken in the
Scripture concerning this gift, and I have come to
Him, my heavenly Father, to receive it. He has promised not to give me a 'stone when I ask for bread'
(Matt. 7:9). Therefore I can be confident that what
I am speaking is truly His gift of a new tongue. As
you continue to use the gift, you will pass through this
test, and come to the confidence that this gift will
become to you all that Scripture promises.

The second test usually comes after one has exercised the gift for a time—perhaps a few weeks or
months. The initial joy and enthusiasm which one
had in the use of the gift begins to fade. You can still
speak in tongues as fluently as ever, but it doesn't seem
to be 'doing' anything for you. It's just a hollow shell,
with no inner content. The temptation is to let the gift
fall into disuse. This is a temptation which one must
resolutely resist. Every gift of God involves a steward-
ship of that gift. One who receives the gift of tongues
must *from the beginning* take this stance: God has
given me a gift which I shall use to worship Him *all
the rest of my life.*

There is actually a good reason *why* God allows
the initial enthusiasm to wane. He does not want our

use of this gift to be grounded on the shifting sands of our own feelings, but upon the solid rock of His Word. "I do not pray in tongues because it gives me a continual thrill, but because His Word has given me some specific promises concerning the exercise of this gift: For example, it edifies me, I utter mysteries unto God, I give thanks well. Regardless of what I feel or don't feel, the Bible tells me plainly that the exercise of this gift will have positive results. I believe the Word!"

God wants us to grow to the point where we act according to faith rather than feelings. The great blessing of speaking in tongues is found in its regular and disciplined use over a long period of time—months and years—and not in the passing emotion of a few prayer sessions. It is a tool of prayer which is self-sharpening and improves with use!

GOING ON

One who receives the gift of tongues often develops a healthy spiritual appetite! He wants to know more and more about 'living in the Spirit.' This appetite needs to be satisfied with solid, well-prepared nourishment.

Chief on the diet, of course, is the study of Scripture itself. A "Daily Quiet Time with God" is indispensable to sound spiritual growth. (See suggested procedure on page 136.)

Our spiritual menu may also include books which can help lead us into a deeper and surer walk in the Spirit. It seems that God anticipated this present-day renewal of the gifts and ministries of the Holy Spirit, and 'sent on ahead' some pioneers to chart the way for us. Each believer will be led to certain books which will just 'hit the mark.' However, it does seem that certain writers have been given a special gift for helping people in this aspect of the Christian life, and we recommend three of them to the reader, for further help along the way: Andrew Murray, Watchman Nee, and Hannah Whitall Smith.

Andrew Murray was a Scots Presbyterian missionary to South Africa in the Nineteenth Century. His writings are too numerous to mention in detail, but three or four of his books will give the reader a good grasp of his thought: *The Spirit of Christ, Absolute Surrender, The Two Covenants, With Christ in the School of Prayer, Full Blessing of Pentecost.*

Watchman Nee is the product of Western missions in China, and the founder of an indigenous movement in his homeland. After a long period of imprisonment under the communists, he was cruelly tortured and martyred for the Faith. His books, *The Normal Christian Life; Sit, Walk, Stand;* and *The Release of the Spirit* offer many insights into the Spirit-led walk.

Hannah Whitall Smith was a Quaker who wrote the classic *The Christian's Secret of a Happy Life.* It, too, offers many helpful insights for the person who seeks to follow the pathway of discipleship.

Recommending these books does not mean that one agrees with everything that is written, or that all parts of their writing are equally helpful. All of us "see in part." But, taken as a whole, these are fellow Christians who have gone before us, whom we may recommend as faithful guides.

For the Body

Martin Luther, commenting on Mark 16:17, 18, said, "The signs here spoken of [including that of speaking in tongues], are to be used *according to need.* When the need arises, and the Gospel is hard pressed,

then we must definitely do these signs, before we allow
the Gospel to be maligned and knocked down."

I believe that we are in such a time as Luther
alluded to. The Scripture gives us every reason to
believe that in such a time the Lord will give added
power, yes, added gifts—to help His Church meet the
challenge. Not only speaking in tongues, but *every*
gift mentioned in Scripture, is for our day. It is not
for us to question the value of these gifts. The fact
that they are gifts from Christ is reason enough to
desire them earnestly, for surely He would not give
His people worthless gifts. It is for us to determine
from Scripture what *His* thinking is concerning each
gift, and then to use it accordingly.

As a Lutheran pastor, ordained to 'tend the flock
of God which is my charge,' I want these gifts to be
protected from human and carnal abuse; I also want
them to be protected from *dis*use, through timidity,
fear, or misunderstanding. And I believe that these
two extremes—abuse and disuse—are both dealt with
effectually when we see these manifestations not as
a gimmick or a toy given to an individual believer, but
as a ministry and a blessing set into the Body of
Christ by God (I Cor. 12:28).

When these manifestations of the Holy Spirit are
subject to mature pastoral guidance and discipline
within the congregation, there will be no lack of decency and order in our midst. And on the other hand,
there will be no quenching of the Spirit when these
manifestations are earnestly desired, prayed for, and
then welcomed—not merely as a blessing for an individual, but as a needed blessing and enduement for
the Body of Christ.

In these chapters we have tried to make a case
for speaking in tongues. Not because it is the greatest
gift, but because it is usually deemed the least. If the

Church cannot come to terms with this so-called 'least of the gifts,' on the level of actual experience and practice, can we really come to terms with the other gifts, except in a theoretical way? Can we expect God to pour out His power upon the Church—power which the Church needs so desperately in this day—if we are not ready in our hearts to accept this, too? If we say in effect, "Lord, give us Thy Holy Spirit—but no tongues, please!" have we not thereby prevented God from answering our prayer, by setting up our own conditions? May it not be that in this day of ours—a day languishing under an oppressive cloud of anti-supernaturalism—a day when anyone who speaks of miracles is looked upon as somewhat antiquated or queer—a day when many would bring all things, even the Word of God, before the bar of human reason—may it not be that in such a day as this, our God, whose foolishness is still wiser than the wisdom of men—may it not be that He has gone into His store-house of gifts, dusted off one which has lain in general disuse for a time, and comes now to His people, the Church, and invites them to receive a gift which will be nothing but foolishness to the proud or carnal mind, but to the Body of Christ it will be the very blessing which Christ himself intended when He poured out His Spirit on the Day of Pentecost: "and they all spoke in other tongues, as the Spirit gave them utterance"?

Appendix

How to Have a Daily
Quiet Time with God

One of Jesus' parting commands to His disciples was this: *"Make disciples* of all the nations" (Matt. 28:19). The word 'disciple' comes from the same root as the word 'discipline.' A disciple is not just a curious or casual follower of Jesus, but a *disciplined follower*. This is what Jesus wants us to be.

To achieve something worthwhile always requires discipline. No person ever mastered a musical instrument without the discipline of regular practice. Every athlete submits to rigorous disciplines in order to excel in his chosen sport. A lawyer, doctor, housewife, mechanic, secretary, student, engineer—each must follow prescribed disciplines in order to excel. Isn't it reasonable to believe that we must also follow *spiritual disciplines* in order to excel as Christians? If we follow regular disciplines to excel in a profession, a sport, a hobby—which prepare us only for this life—shouldn't we much more follow strict disciplines which prepare us for eternity? No discipline will pay greater dividends. "The things that are seen are transient, but the things that are unseen are eternal" (II Cor. 4:18).

The Christian religion is essentially an *experience*— a personal experience of God. Theology and doctrine are simply an explanation of that experience. Many people know something about the doctrine, but have never really had the experience. So of course their religion is dry, formal, powerless. It has no life, no

136

zest, no sense of reality. "This is eternal life, that they might *know* thee, the only true God, and Jesus Christ whom thou hast sent" (John 17:3).

The simple discipline suggested on the next pages can change all that. It can lead you into a living experience of God. It is *a daily quiet time with God.* Every great Christian has followed a discipline similar to the one suggested here. No Christian can afford to bypass this *basic spiritual discipline.* It is gloriously simple. Yet it is astonishingly effective. We challenge you to put it into practice faithfully for *one month.* Even in that short time you will see the potential it has to literally *change your life.* "For the word of God is living and active" (Heb. 4:12).

WHAT DO I NEED?

1. A Bible.
2. A notebook (preferably a small loose-leaf which you can carry about with you).
3. A pen or pencil.
4. A quiet place.
5. A definite time set aside each day—at least 15 minutes to begin with. (It can easily grow to an hour!) The early morning is usually the best time. Make it the same time each day, whenever possible.

WHAT IS THE PROCEDURE?

1. Realize that God is with you in your quiet time. He stands ready not only to meet with you, but actually to guide and direct you. "When the Spirit of truth [the Holy Spirit] comes, he will guide you into all the truth" (John 16:13). How does God come to you? He comes to you principally through His Word, the Bible. This is the channel which the Holy Spirit uses most frequently.

2. Begin with a brief prayer. Thank God for His special blessings to you and for being here with you *now*. Tell Him that you believe—you are expecting—that He will meet with you, speak to you, and reveal His will to you through this quiet time. "You will seek me and find me; when you seek me with all your heart, I will be found by you, says the Lord" (Jer. 29:13, 14).

3. Read the brief passage of Scripture which you have chosen for the day. (See Scripture suggestions, page 141.)

   a. Do not read simply to 'understand.' Read with a feeling of 'openness' and 'receptivity.' You are 'feeding' on God's Word. It is spiritual food to you. "Man shall not live by bread alone, but by every word that proceeds from the mouth of God" (Matt. 4:4).

   b. You will not understand everything you read. Don't let that bother you. Take it in. Whisper to God, "I don't get all of this . . . but I know that You will help me to understand as we move along." "The fear [reverence] of the Lord is the beginning of knowledge" (Prov. 1:7).

   c. Let your reading be broken up by moments of prayer and meditation. In other words, *enjoy* this spiritual meal. Taste it. Savor it. Read parts of it out loud to hear how it sounds with differing emphases.

4. Write down what comes to you during this reading-meditating-praying time. THIS IS THE KEY TO YOUR WHOLE QUIET TIME. When you write down, you begin to crystalize and capture the actual workings of the Holy Spirit in your heart, mind,

and soul. Make it quite personal and direct. Not simply what the passage 'means,' but what it means *to and for you.* Perhaps it will trigger some thought not directly related to the passage you are reading. That's all right. Write it down. *This is the Holy Spirit's personal message to you.*

a. Naturally you are not always 'tuned in' to the Holy Spirit 100 percent—you will get some 'static' from your own thoughts and opinions. But more and more, *as you faithfully follow this daily discipline,* your little notebook will become a record of God's personal dealing with your own life.

b. Here is an actual sample of someone's quiet time record for one day: "June 3rd. The Lord's Prayer. The Apostles' Creed. Romans 6:22–23. Now that I am set free from sin and become a slave of God, my return is sanctification and its end, eternal life. For the wages of sin is death, but the free gift of God is eternal life in Christ Jesus, our Lord. It's a good feeling to rid ourselves of sin, to feel clean and in God's good graces everlastingly. How can we know and learn of God without the will to do so? This I think of so much of late. But what joy it brings to know we have our heavenly Father, our living God, to go to. We give thanks to Thee, yes, more than thanks, O Lord our God, for all Thy goodness. Amen."

5. Close with a time of prayer.

a. Begin with thanks, praise, adoration.

b. Confess your sins, asking God's forgiveness.

c. Affirm your faith in God. Say at least several strong statements of faith. For example—"God

is my refuge and strength! . . . I know that Jesus
Christ is alive, and His Kingdom is surely coming; it will come to me today! . . . I can do all
things through Christ who strengthens me! . . .
With God nothing shall be impossible! . . . The
Lord is my shepherd! . . . He leadeth me, O blessed thought!"

d. Present to God your petitions and requests. You
   may want to keep a prayer-list, and check them
   off as God answers them. Don't be satisfied with
   unanswered prayer. Jesus said, "Whatever you
   ask in prayer, believe that you are receiving it
   and you will" (Mark 11:24). Keep the list small
   enough so you can pray for each need with real
   purpose and faith.

OTHER POINTS

1. A Daily Quiet Time with God is one spiritual discipline—one of the most important—but still only one.
   If your life as a Christian is to mature in a healthy
   way, you will want to observe other basic disciplines
   as well. These can be carried out most effectively
   within the framework of your own local church:

   a. Regular church attendance.

   b. Regular Bible study under a qualified Bible teach-
      er.

   c. Regular giving to the Lord's work (ten percent
      of your income).

   d. Regular work or service for the Lord under the
      supervision of those placed over you in the Lord.

2. Divide your notebook into two sections. The first
   section is to record your Daily Quiet Time. In the

second section you take notes on sermons, lectures, Bible studies, radio talks, thoughts that come to you during the day—anything of spiritual value. In order to integrate these notes into your life in a practical way, convert them into a prayer during your next quiet time. In other words, take the substance of the notes and boil it down into a prayer. Apply it to your own life.

WHERE SHOULD I START IN THE BIBLE?

1. One of the simplest methods for selecting your daily Bible passage is to read through a single book, a few verses each day. The Gospel of John, Colossians, the Epistle of James, and the First Epistle of John are good ones to begin with.

2. You may want to follow certain themes, such as salvation, forgiveness, healing, etc. If so, use a Bible concordance to find different passages dealing with your theme.

3. Another way to begin would be to use the following series of Bible passages, which will lead you through some basic Christian teachings in a systematic way. Some can be covered in a single day; others might be worth spending several days on:

   a. The "new life" of a Christian. I John 5:9–13, James 1:2–8, James 1:19–26, I John 1:5–10, Mark 8:34–38, Eph. 2:1–10, I Pet. 1:3–9, I Pet. 1:22—2:3, John 15:1–11, II Cor. 5:14–21.

   b. Christian responsibility. Phil. 4:4–13, I Pet. 3: 8–17, Rom. 14:13–23, Col. 3:16–25, Gal. 6:1–10.

   c. Adventuring in the Psalms. Psalms 1, 8, 73, 32, 46, 139, 91, 22.